SELF-COMPASSION
FOR TEENS

129
Activities & Practices to Cultivate Kindness

Lee-Anne Gray, PsyD

Praise for
Self-Compassion for Teens

"For a teen, self-compassion opens the door to loving and gratifying relationships, the full unfolding of intelligence, and deep wellbeing in all domains. In this groundbreaking book, Dr. Lee-Anne Gray offers the most clear, thorough and accessible guidance in teaching teens self-compassion that I have encountered or could imagine. My prayer is that anyone who is engaged with teens find their way to this book; the ripples will awaken consciousness everywhere."

- **Tara Brach PhD** ,
Author *Radical Acceptance* and *True Refuge*

"This book is just the ticket for parents, teachers, and counselors who know the burdens of modern teens and want to help. Self-compassion is a core emotional skill that builds emotional resilience. In this book, Dr. Gray offers a wide array of exercises that awaken self-compassion in teens, tailored specifically for challenging situations such as school stress, identity and body image problems, substance abuse, anxiety, autism and chronic illness. Written in a clear and compassionate style, caregivers will discover a powerful new approach to tricky problems. Highly recommended!"

- **Christopher Germer, PhD**,
Author, *The Mindful Path to Self-Compassion*

"Self-compassion is one of the most important strengths for teenagers to develop to support resilience, well-being, and social connection. And yet it can be quite difficult to talk about and teach. Dr. Lee-Anne Gray has created an extraordinary resource for those who want to cultivate self-compassion in themselves and others. This book provides practical exercises, discussion prompts, and a deep dive into what it truly means to care about ourselves. I have not seen a better resource for teaching self-compassion, not just for teenagers, but for anyone."

- **Kelly McGonigal, PhD**,
Author, *The Upside of Stress*

"An exquisite collection of powerful practices that parents, teachers, and therapists can all share with the teens in their lives."

- **Christopher Willard, PsyD**,
Author, *Growing Up Mindful*

"Among the keys to self-compassion, Lee-Anne Gray teaches, are mindful awareness, inner strength, and self-regulation. In this succinct manual, parents, teachers and clinicians are guided to impart these and other essential qualities to young people. It is guidance sorely needed in our culture."

- **Gabor Maté, MD**,
Author, *Scattered: How Attention Deficit Disorder Originates*
And What You Can Do About It

"*Self-Compassion for Teens* provides a treasure trove of nurturing, compassionate activities for teens, professionals, and parents to help transform lives. Dr. Gray's clear, tender-hearted, and caring approach shows a depth of understanding critically needed in reaching the souls of our youth and making a real difference. An invaluable asset to every library."

- **Charlotte Reznick, PhD**,
Author, *The Power of Your Child's Imagination:*
How to Transform Stress and Anxiety into Joy and Success

"*Self-Compassion for Teens* is a wonderful collection of practices and activities inspiring teens to treat themselves kindly. For teens dealing with anxiety, depression, ADHD, school challenges, and much more—this book offers new insights that increase self-acceptance. What an important resource for clinicians, teachers, parents and teens to promote self-kindness, creativity, and empathy."

- **Scott Barry Kaufman, PhD**,
Author, *Ungifted: Intelligence Redefined*

"*Self-Compassion for Teens* is a book that will help many teenagers improve their quality of life by reducing negative emotions, such as anxiety, frustration, worry, and stress, etc. It will help them develop self-compassion, as well as compassion for others. This book has each topic laid out with three categories: Learn, Practice, and Reflect, and is written in easily understood, simple language."

- **Venerable Tenzin Yignyen**,
Faculty Hobart & William Smith Colleges

Published by
PESI Publishing & Media
PESI, Inc
3839 White Ave
Eau Claire, WI 54703

Cover: Al Postlewaite
Editing: Marietta Whittelsey
Layout: Bookmasters & Amy Rubenzer

ISBN: 9781683730255

Printed in the United States of America.

PESI
Publishing
& Media
www.pesipublishing.com

Dedication

This book is dedicated to
everyone suffering from *Educational Trauma*.

Contents

Acknowledgments

First, and foremost, I want to thank Meg Mickelson Graf for taking the time to learn about my work, and for introducing me to Linda Jackson and Karsyn Morse at PESI Publishing & Media. Sincerest thanks to Karsyn for visioning this work for me, and to Linda for publishing it.

Special thanks goes out to Eric Medina, PsyD, for many dialogues on the definition and nature of self-empathy. Likewise, I am grateful to Edwin Rutsch, director of the Center for Building a Culture of Empathy, for our empathy buddy sessions, which have been an essential component of my own self-care practices, and in teasing out the spectrum of empathy.

There are many teens I've encountered over the course of my professional life; one stands out for his willingness to be interviewed for this book. Aaron Faraj is credited with sharing his wisdom with me. He helped me tap into unique considerations by trusting me with his inner truths.

Everyone I encounter becomes my teacher, however, one specific teacher stands out for the enormous impact she has had on me as a mindfulness educator and parent. Traca Gress deeply influenced my capacity to hold vast space, practice powerful breathing techniques, and use the intensely mind-expanding bija mantras.

Charlotte Reznick, PhD, is a child psychologist and very close confidante. Her book, *The Power of Your Child's Imagination*, has been an inspirational teacher to me in many ways, and influences some self-compassion practices in this book. When I secretly dreamed of writing a book, Charlotte supported me and helped me learn about the world of publishing. She helped me crystallize ideas, and flow with the ups and downs of the writing experience. Thank you, Charlotte, for being a loving presence in my life, and for being a role model of ongoing self-compassion practice.

There are many people who contributed to the emergence of this book whom I also wish to acknowledge. To Al Postelwaite: You captured the whimsical and ever-unfolding nature of adolescence in the cover design, and I am so thrilled and grateful! To Marietta Whittelsey, thank you for catching my typos, and clarifying the content. A big and heartfelt thank you to Amy Rubenzer for capturing self-empathy and mirror neurons with fun and heart-full designs! There are others too, at PESI, who contributed to this book while supporting my seminars of the same title —Thanks to Catie Cox, Shannon Becker, Kayla Huset, Nick Theis, and others who help me bring self-compassion to more teens.

I extend infinite love and gratitude to my family and friends. Two friends were particularly helpful when it came to practical life matters, encouragement, and relentless faith in me: Dena Lazar and Wendy Taira. To my beloved Richard, thank you for giving me the space to cultivate self-compassion, compassion, self-empathy, empathy, and more. I cherish the love and goodness you bring to my life. To my beautiful and healthy children, who are also my co-learners and main sources of inspiration and passion-filled education: Lewis, Chase, and Zoe, thank you for your love, and commitment to practicing self-compassion, compassion, self-empathy, and empathy. You inspire me always, and promote amazing passion!

About the Author

Lee-Anne Gray, PsyD, is a clinical and forensic psychologist and P21 educator. She is certified in EMDR, a trauma treatment, as well as a national speaker and expert in special education, mindful awareness, assessment, and gifted individuals. As the president and CEO of The Connect Group, she currently serves the global educational community with innovative professional development seminars in empathy, compassion cultivation, Design Thinking, and transformational coaching.

Prior to this, Dr. Gray was supervising psychologist at the largest special education nonprofit organization in the nation. She also enjoyed a thriving private practice where she used EMDR to promote peak performance in students, families, professional athletes, and high-performing executives. She is formerly an instructor of Psychology of Gender in the Departments of Psychology/Women's Studies at UCLA. Dr. Gray is a contributing author to *Pedagogies of Kindness and Respect*, where she discussed *Educational Trauma* and *Empathic Education for a Compassionate Nation* (*EECN*). Along with young people as equal participants, Dr. Gray cofounded and codesigned EECN (a democratic educational model, shaped by Design Thinking), piloted as The Connect Group School. The Connect Group School is an example of students practicing self-compassion as one way of mitigating and healing Educational Trauma.

Introduction

WHY IS SELF-COMPASSION FOR TEENS IMPORTANT?

Teens are suffering from relationship difficulties, body image problems, concentration issues, school pressure, parental criticism, teacher demands, substance abuse, anxiety, depression, and eating disorders, as well as the challenges associated with emerging adulthood identity. School is intended to train people in how to live healthy, happy, and productive lives, however, current educational practices deprive students of the time, space, and opportunities needed to learn about themselves. Worse yet, many students are traumatized by archaic educational practices that promote cyclical and systemic human problems. *Educational Trauma* is a spectrum of events that victimize students, parents, and educators. On the mildest end, it is the anxiety students feel around test pressures and standardized academic expectations. This anxiety can also be experienced by parents and educators for different reasons, and is the result of placing maladaptive pressures on youngsters and their caregivers. Educational Trauma increases in severity with many other events that cause harm and long-term consequences, such as: the use of stimulant medication to control atypical student behavior, the use of criminal justice to discipline students of color in low-income public schools, and the school-to-prison pipeline. Teens need guidance in how to face and identify pain and suffering. Not just for their own sake and self-care practice, but also to respond and care for others in moments of pain. The practices in this book offer immediate and actionable ways of helping teens confront hardships with the confidence that even very difficult problems deserve the willingness to attempt resolution. With educational practices contributing to student distress, there is an urgent need for these types of tools, skills, and practices so teens can thrive, even in very challenging situations.

Let us be clear that self-compassion is promoted with the intention to extend compassion to others once one's needs are adequately sated. Thinking about the airplane attendant's instructions prior to take-off: "When traveling with small children, or those in need of assistance, please place the oxygen mask on yourself first—then help your traveling companion." Self-compassion is the act of putting the proverbial oxygen facemask on your own face first, so you can help others. There are many who would say it is easier to give to others than it is to give to themselves. This concept relates to the power of self-compassion in amplifying compassion for others. When we prioritize the needs and suffering of others over our own, we essentially limit our helpfulness to others in their moments of need. By not placing the proverbial oxygen mask on ourselves first, we only have a limited amount of oxygen/energy to help others before petering out. Teaching self-compassion practices to teens empowers them to set boundaries, care for themselves, cope with the intensity of suffering, and take action to relieve their own suffering so that they may serve others too.

The activities contained in this practice book are associated with decreased symptoms of depression, and increased life satisfaction. Research (Neff, 2011) demonstrates that self-compassion increases resilience and well-being, while decreasing depression and anxiety. Adolescents benefit from training in self-compassion because it gives them tools for seeing moments of suffering with open, balanced attention and kindness to themselves. It cultivates curiosity about oneself, and strengthens neuronal connections that promote health and healing. Self-compassion teaches teens that their moments of suffering are commonly felt by others, thereby reducing some of the isolating and painful moments common in adolescence. *Self-Compassion for Teens* is a collection of activities, practice sheets, and self-reflections that train teens in a foundation for kindness to themselves and others. The way we treat ourselves inevitably influences how we are with others, and therefore self-compassion contributes to healthier relationships. Many teens really want a good friend, who is always right there with them. Practicing self-compassion reveals this inner best friend, and reminds us of Ghandi's words: "Be the change you wish to see in the world." When we train teens to treat themselves well, they in turn treat others well, and create communities that are friendly to everyone. Self-compassionate teens may represent the healthiest future outlook for mitigating Educational Trauma, and for this reason it is timely and urgent to share this work with teens in your life.

HOW WILL TEACHERS, PARENTS, AND CLINICIANS BENEFIT FROM THIS WORK?

The launching of teens into adulthood is becoming an increasingly problematic stage of development for North American families. Teens are suffering from trauma, pressure, and committing suicide as a result (Gray, 2013). Students who succeed in high school and enter college are failing to complete college at alarming rates. Students who make it to college are finding themselves too burned out to complete their degrees. This is far worse for students of color, and those living in poverty. One response to this depth of suffering is a tendency for children to rely on their parents (or public assistance programs) for longer than in earlier generations, and to return to live in the family home after years away. The suffering that begins in the teen years impacts future functioning, as well as the health and prosperity of families and communities. The techniques and tools in this book are short and easy to apply, teachings that promote adolescents' academic success and healthy launching into adulthood. Parents, educators, and clinicians need to promote self-compassion in teens because it increases positivity, leads others to be happy too, and creates a framework for holding positive and negative feelings/experiences at once. This practical book offers many activities, meditations, and practices that heal trauma, widen emotional capacity, promote healthy sexual and gender development, improve executive functioning, and increase overall happiness. Teaching self-compassion to teens is one way of loving them, while training them to love and heal themselves. It represents an example of "teacherly love," a concept integrating the essence of teachers, parents, and helping professionals who care for young people (Goldstein, 1997).

HOW TO USE THIS BOOK

Jump in! Yes, anywhere! You can turn to the table of contents, select the chapter you're most interested in, and begin there. If your teen is traumatized, start with Chapter 8 and the **Self-Compassion Training Protocol for Traumatized Teens**, otherwise you can begin anywhere.

If you're a parent, and you have a struggling teen, consider using these activities, only in times when your teen is calm, well-regulated, and personally engaged in the practice. These activities build skills when practiced in moments of peace. (Very few practices are designed for moments of crisis.) This practice book is not intended to de-escalate crisis moments, however training in self-compassion can reduce the frequency and duration of difficult moments.

As an educator, including relevant activities from this workbook in your classroom routine will cultivate social emotional skills in your students, while fostering the resilience needed to be successful in school.

If you're a clinician, and your next patient is struggling with substance abuse, for example, turn to any page in Chapter 10, and voilà, you'll have interventions, practice sheets, and activities you can use right then and there.

This practice book is a complete collection designed for use by adults training teens in the cultivation of self-compassion. While you can implement each activity in isolation, no one chapter, nor the entire workbook, is intended as a complete treatment/training program. These activities are supplemental tools to be used with other interventions and/or plans. This practice book is intended for three audiences, and has two parts.

Three Audiences

FIRST, this practice book is equally approachable by parents, educators, and clinicians. For parents, you can use these activities in the whole family for greatest impact. Parents, these activities have been adapted from many adult activities and described in ways appropriate to different teen populations. Since self-compassion practices are also components of healthy approaches to parenting, it benefits whole families when just one parent commits to and cultivates self-compassion. Feel free to use any of the activities in this practice book yourself. I do!

SECOND, educators represent one of the groups affected by *Educational Trauma*, with the unique position of having their jobs and sustainability threatened by policy and practices. Educators need compassion because the allure of a teaching career has morphed into a source of abuse. In her 2008 book, *White Chalk Crime*, Karen Horwitz details the horrific teacher abuses she collected from educators nationwide. Educators who use the practices in this book themselves, and/or with their students, create a classroom environment that is kind and respectful, wholesome, and healthy. It is the opposite of the environments that breed bullying, while simultaneously healing educators, and their students, who've encountered *Educational Trauma*. Self-compassion practices in classrooms offer all those stressed and hurting by school procedures an opportunity to begin healing. Healing the self heals the world.

THIRD, this workbook is an effective companion for clinicians working with teens. Clinicians include a wide range of professionals who care for youngsters, such as: speech and language pathologists, occupational therapists, psychotherapists, psychiatrists, social workers, and more. The activities build essential skills such as mindful awareness, executive functioning, social skills, as well as coping and self-regulation abilities. Kindness toward oneself and realizing that humans everywhere suffer, just like we do, has a healing effect. When clinicians practice these activities alone, and/or with their patients, they cultivate more compassion in the world too. **Some activities and worksheets are designed to be given directly to teens to complete.**

Two Parts

This workbook is divided into two parts. **PART I is a three chapter summary of the foundational aspects of training teens in self-compassion.** First, terms such as *self-compassion* and *compassion*, *empathy* and *self-empathy*, *self-criticism*, and *self-esteem* are explored in order to reframe certain maladaptive behaviors as universal expressions of suffering. Teens are subjected to harsh controls, pressure, and punishments that most adults would never tolerate in their families, nor in the workplace. This has significant impact on the developing brain, as evidenced in the Adverse Childhood Experiences study (Anda & Filetti, 1997). Chapter 2 explores the interpersonal neurobiology of self-compassion, specifically how it affects the developing adolescent brain and interpersonal relationships. The third chapter explores the unique challenges of launching from adolescence to adulthood, as well as the special considerations associated with training teens in self-compassion. For example, affect management in the presence of positive and negative experiences is critical to moving into independent adulthood. Training teens in self-compassion has the added benefit of expanding coping skills by dealing directly with pain and suffering.

PART II contains chapters devoted to training teens, from diverse populations and/or with special conditions, in self-compassion. Chapter 4 begins the section by addressing a variety of challenges common in high schools. From bullying to test anxiety, school pressures, parental expectations, and teacher criticism, teens face a lot of stress. Chapter 4 is packed with activities most teens can benefit from when managing their academic programs. Chapter 5 delves more specifically into anxiety and depression, as they are quickly becoming epidemic experiences. Robust research findings reveal that self-compassionate people tend to be less depressed and anxious (Neff, 2011). As such, self-compassion training is a natural, noninvasive, and inexpensive treatment option for teens suffering from depression and anxiety. Chapter 6 addresses the issues faced by teens diagnosed with or facing attention and hyperactivity concerns. It offers activities and tools to reframe student experiences without pathologizing them. Understanding oneself in a positive light is an act of self-kindness that reduces suffering associated with ADHD. Mindful awareness practices increase mental control and executive functioning, while reducing the need for medication in some students.

Chapter 7 continues Part II with a perspective on the body image concerns and eating disorders that arise in the teen years. Bringing mindfulness to eating, and kindness to cultural values that strain teens' relationships to their bodies, can improve image concerns while reducing maladaptive eating patterns. Chapter 8 explores the unique precautions needed when training traumatized teens in self-compassion. The ever-present risk of dissociation and decompensation require the use of the Self-Compassion Training Protocol for Traumatized Teens. In Chapter 9, the self-compassion practices and activities are specifically designed with LGBTQ teens in mind. The introduction of the spectrums and fluidity of both gender and sexuality are explored in order to promote self-compassion. Chapter 10 is an assortment of tools to be used with teens who are abusing substances to self-soothe. Later in Chapter 11, self-compassion with teens who have autism is explored. While limited by the capacity to communicate, it is possible to train teens with autism in self-compassion. It focuses on self-regulation, reframing complex stereotypic mannerisms, and managing atypical play and interaction patterns with kindness to self. Chapter 12 concludes the workbook with activities that can be used with teens who are chronically or terminally ill. It explores concepts of death, dying, and legacy as means of easing the suffering associated with serious medical conditions. The practice book concludes with the reminder that changing the world begins when we work on changing ourselves. Healing *Educational Trauma* arises when self-healing is initiated; a self-compassion practice that begins in adolescence is one way to do so.

1 What Is Self-Compassion?

Self-compassion is the cultivation of qualities of friendliness towards oneself. There are four components to cultivating self-compassion:

1. **Mindful awareness**

2. **Kindness to ourselves** (metta: loving kindness and willingness to take action to relieve suffering)

3. **Shared humanity**

4. **The willingness to act to relieve suffering**

The following five activities promote each of the components mentioned previously, and form the basic foundation of cultivating self-compassion:

1. **Selective Attention** (preparatory activity for 25 Breaths, or any other mindfulness meditation)

2. **25 Breaths**

3. **Watching Thoughts and Feelings**

4. **Loving Kindness**

5. **Just Like Me. . .**

(1.) SELECTIVE ATTENTION ACTIVITY

Learn

Mindful awareness is an open, balanced way of paying attention. It invites curiosity about what is alive and present in this very moment, while suspending judgment. Our minds are always wandering; by practicing paying attention, concentration and focus can improve substantially. Generally, people seem to think they are paying attention while they are awake, however, research studies indicate we miss a lot of what's going on right in front of us (Simons & Chabris, 1999). Use this optional activity to help teens see the benefit of cultivating mindful awareness skills.

Pre-Practice

Explain to teens: "When people are focused on one thing, they sometimes miss other things happening all around them."

An experiment by Simons & Chabris (1999) asked student subjects to watch a video of people in black or white jerseys playing basketball. The student subjects were asked to count how many times the white team players passed the basketball. While concentrating on the white team, many student subjects missed the person in a gorilla costume wandering onto the scene while a basketball was being tossed around. A search for videos on "selective attention test," will yield videos of this experiment to show your teen. It's fun to watch, if you don't spoil the part about the gorilla, and opens the discussion about what it means to pay attention.

Practice

Then show your teen a video of the experiment mentioned previously, or tell them the story and discuss the questions that follow. https://www.youtube.com/watch?v=vJG698U2Mvo

Reflect

- Did you notice the gorilla while counting ball passes?

- Have there been times when you thought you were paying attention, then realized you really weren't?

- How did it feel when you realized you weren't paying attention?

- Is it dependent on whatever interests you or catches your eye?

2. 25 BREATHS

Learn

There are many ways of increasing mindful awareness skills—often by paying attention to the breath, but not always. Research (Hölzel et al., 1999) shows that practicing activities like 25 Breaths contributes to an increased sense of well-being and peace, while increasing density of gray matter in the hippocampus. This brain area is associated with learning, memory, self-awareness, compassion, and introspection.

Here is one breath awareness activity you can use to help teens increase mindful awareness skills.

Practice

- Explain: Sitting or laying down in a comfortable position, close your eyes, if you feel comfortable doing so.

- You may also focus your gaze softly, and downward on one place in front of you.

- Once settled, focus your attention on your breath.

- Notice it moving in through your nostrils, and down into your lungs.

- Feel your lungs rise and fall with every breath.

- See if you can breathe deeply enough to fill your belly up at least two times.

- Once you are grounded in your body and connected to your breath, count each in-breath and out-breath as one—like this:

  - Inhale—one, exhale—one.
  - Inhale—two, exhale—two.
  - Inhale—three, exhale—three.

- Encourage your teen to continue counting inhale and exhale breaths until they reach twenty-five.

- At twenty-five, count backward—like this:

  - Inhale—twenty-five, exhale—twenty-five.
  - Inhale—twenty-four, exhale—twenty-four.
  - Inhale—twenty-three, exhale—twenty-three . . . and so on, until counting leads right back to one.

- Most people are expected to lose count, and the instruction is to just begin again at number one whenever it happens.

- Reassure your teen that it is okay to lose count; it is precisely how we practice moving our attention back to where we want it. When we do so kindly, and with loving allowance, it becomes much easier to focus for longer periods of time.

- Set a timer and practice 25 Breaths with your teen for two, three, or five minutes depending on how long your teen is willing to practice.

- Even a little bit helps!

- It is very important for your teen to freely choose this practice, and the length of time that is most comfortable to them.

- Increasing the session time gradually is encouraged, however not necessary to reap benefits.

Modification

- For teens with excellent mental control, encourage them to count to a higher number like fifty or one hundred.

- For teens who become proficient with twenty-five breaths, increase it by intervals of twenty-five breaths until they reach one hundred.

- For those having difficulty with twenty-five, start with only ten breaths.

It doesn't matter what number is set as the goal, as long as it does not change mid practice.

Reflect

Dialogue with your teen about what it was like to practice 25 Breaths. Ask the following questions:

- What was it like to focus on your breath and count at the same time?

- Sometimes in the middle of breath-work practices, people suddenly feel like it is pointless. Did that thought arise for you?

- Was your body drawing your attention during the activity?

3. WATCHING THOUGHTS AND FEELINGS

Learn

Mindfulness is achieved through mental training, which teaches us how to calm our busy minds, settle wild and changing emotions, as well as the art of detaching from our very own thoughts. Remind your teen that our thoughts and feelings may seem very real, but they aren't necessarily true. Here is how to train teens to notice thoughts and feelings, while also practicing letting them go.

Practice

- Find a comfortable position.

- If you need to move, this can be a walking practice. Standing is another option. Whichever position draws your attention/preference most, commit to it for a period of 2, 3, or 5 minutes.

- If this activity leaves you feeling uncomfortable at any time, please stop and share your observations.

- Take a deep breath into your belly. Feel the flow of air move into your nostrils, inflating your lungs and belly, before moving upward and out again.

- Take two more deep belly breaths.

- During this short period, set your intention to notice feelings and thoughts that come to your awareness.

- Setting your intention means making a silent mental commitment to do something or be a certain way (more on setting intentions in Chapter 4).

- Try to remain unattached to the thoughts and feelings that arise. There may be many; there may be few. Just allow and watch.

- Imagine you are watching a movie in your mind's eye. The movie is made up of thoughts and feelings that come and go.

- It's okay to suddenly feel like you have to go do something—anything—other than this activity. See if you can resist the temptation to do whatever else is more appealing.

- When a feeling arises, silently say to yourself, "Right now, I am feeling an emotion."

- Try to resist examining the feeling, finding the source, and/or allowing yourself to feel it too deeply. Remember this is an activity in mental training.

- Thoughts and feelings could arise; the objective is to notice them.

- When a thought arises, silently say to yourself, "Right now, I am thinking."

- While this may seem pointless and boring, it is a very effective way to learn to control your own mind.

Reflect

- How was it to label your thoughts and emotions for a few minutes?

- Were there a lot of thoughts/feelings?

LOVING AND KIND FRIENDLY WISHES (METTA)

Learn

According to Sharon Salzberg (2002), the practice of loving kindness is the first step toward compassion, and involves recognizing oneself, and expressing love and kindness to oneself, as well as for others too. Salzberg says it is the ultimate form of love, kindness, and friendship to pay undivided attention to others. When we turn that attention to ourselves in good times, and especially in times of suffering, it heals while building balance and strength. Research demonstrates that people who practice metta for just seven weeks experience less depressive symptoms, less bias, less migraines and emotional tension, along with increased gray matter, and increased life satisfaction.

Affirm for your teen (and yourself) that it is not self-centered to think about your own happiness, well-being, wealth, wisdom, and peace. Doing so causes neurons in the brain to signal in unique patterns or "brain signatures." The more those patterns are activated, the more habitual they become, which makes happiness, health, wisdom, and well-being a regular way of life.

Practice

Tell teens:

"Repeat the following loving and kind friendly wishes, silently to yourself."

- May I be healthy

- May I be happy

- May I be safe

- May I be peaceful

- May I live easily

Remind teens new to practicing mindful awareness techniques that it is normal for the mind to have many thoughts and be distracted from the friendly wishes. When this happens, teens need to know it is okay to be off task from metta practice, and to gently and kindly return attention to the friendly wishes, resuming the loving kindness practice once again.

Set a timer and practice sending friendly wishes to yourself with your teen. Spend 2, 5, or 10 minutes, whatever feels right for your teen.

Modification

The Loving and Kind Friendly Wishes (Metta) activity may be practiced with others in mind, after practiced repeatedly for oneself. Usually in this order:

- Self

- Benefactor, mentor, or role model (i.e., Dalai Lama)

- Loved one

- Neutral party

- Person with whom there is conflict

- All beings everywhere

When having difficulty with another person, teens may reduce their own suffering by sending Loving and Kind Friendly Wishes to the other person, after using the "Along With Me. . ." practice. Though challenging to send kindness to people with whom we are in conflict, it softens us to do so, thereby reducing our suffering. The Buddha said, "Holding on to anger is like grasping a hot coal with the intent of throwing it at someone else; you are the one who gets burned." Remind your teen that the other person may not even be aware of the pain felt, and so taking action within soothes and heals while reducing conflict.

Reflect

After many silent repetitions, ask teens to discuss what it is like for them to send themselves friendly wishes.

- Would it be any different if they were sending their friends or loved ones friendly wishes?

- Invite teens to practice sending friendly wishes to someone they love, and then comparing the experiences of sending them to yourself as opposed to a loved one.

- Invite teens to practice metta for themselves on a daily basis for maximum effect.

5. "ALONG WITH ME. . ."

Learn

"Along with me. . ." is a practice that promotes awareness of shared humanity, particularly with regard to everyone's desire to be happy and free of suffering. It is the antidote to "Why Me" Syndrome. Whenever you encounter a teen who is struggling with feeling alone, and in pain, practicing this activity may help remind him or her just how interconnected we all are. When we are reminded of being connected with others in times of suffering, it can activate oxytocin, which is associated with closeness, feelings of warmth and attachment. It's been called the "Hug Hormone," "Moral Molecule," "Cuddle Chemical," and "Love Hormone" because it increases through connection with others, while promoting fond fraternal feelings, moral drives, and overall joy. This practice contributes to rewiring the brain for improved attachment, and/or healing from attachment wounds.

This practice is suitable for both groups and individuals.

Practice

When teens are settled in a group (or individually with you), invite them to go around the room (or in their mind), and for each person they see, say:

"Along with me, _____ wants to be happy." (Fill in the blank with the name of the person the teen is looking at, or imagining in her or his mind's eye.)

"Along with me _____ wants to be free of harm."

Repeat the phrase:

"Along with me, _____ wishes to be happy and safe." for everyone in the room, or in the individual teen's mind.

- Invite individual teens to think of their peers, siblings, family members, parents, teachers, etc., bringing each one clearly to mind before silently saying the phrase over and over again.

- For an individual teen, this activity is also beneficial when focusing on just one person, and repeating the phrase several times.

- Ideally, this activity would be introduced and practiced during moments of calm centeredness, to be called on during moments of need. It is unlikely to be beneficial as a method of diffusing crisis, if introduced for the first time during a crisis.

Reflect

- What is it like to concentrate on how others also want to be happy, just like you?

- When I say, "We are all interconnected," what comes to mind?

6. WHAT IS COMPASSION? HOW IS IT DIFFERENT FROM SELF-COMPASSION?

Learn

Self-compassion has an element of common humanity, and directly influences the level of compassion we are capable of showing to others. Dr. Thupten Jinpa, the translator for the Dalai Lama, described compassion as a natural sense of concern in the presence of someone else's needs or suffering, and a desire or resolve to contribute to that person's relief. He identifies three aspects of compassion:

1. Awareness borne out of mindfully paying attention

2. Empathy: the emotional connection to others

3. Motivation: the impulse to act

According to Stanford University's Center for Compassion and Altruism Research and Education, compassion is defined as the ability to recognize suffering in others, and the willingness to act to relieve it. This working definition holds two parts:

1. Recognition of suffering

2. Willingness to act

Conversely, self-compassion is comprised of three components: (a) mindful awareness, (b) kindness to self, (c) common humanity, all of which also create the foundation for compassion toward others. When we cultivate open, balanced attention (mindful awareness), we increase our capacity to perceive suffering. Being kind to oneself sets the tone for being kind to others, and common humanity reminds us that in suffering we are still connected to others, rather than separate and alone. Taken together, these are also the basic skills for recognizing suffering in others, and being willing to act to relieve it.

⑦ GIVING AND RECEIVING COMPASSION

Learn

Some people feel more comfortable giving compassion than receiving it. There is a good feeling that comes with giving, and a vulnerable feeling that goes along with receiving. The following practice sheet is designed to cue memories and instances of giving and receiving compassion.

Practice

Fill out the worksheet on the next page.

Modification

For groups:

- Sit in dyads/triads/quads as appropriate to the number of teens in the group.

- Invite each teen to connect with the experience of giving/receiving compassion.

- Each person takes 2 minutes to describe the experience of giving/receiving the compassion recalled in the direction mentioned previously.

- Others listen without speaking.

- At the end of 2 minutes, the "listeners" get 2 minutes each to reflect back what they heard.

- Listeners do not have to "fill up" all 2 minutes, if he or she has only a little to say. If this is the case, the entire group sits silently until the 2 minutes are up.

- Repeat the exercise until all participants have been heard and reflected back to.

Reflect

- The group modification is a profound practice in teaching individuals respectful, reflective, compassionate listening skills.

Discussion Topics

- What differences did you notice between practicing self-compassion vs. compassion for others?

- Is everyone entitled to compassion?

- How might we offer compassion to people who are very different from us?

Reflect

- Discuss self-esteem and self-criticism.

- Explore the nature of ego, how it is ever changing as we grow, learn, and develop.

- Encourage teens to hold on to their own self-worth regardless of what is happening around them.

GIVING AND RECEIVING COMPASSION

Received compassion from someone else	Gave compassion to someone else	How did it feel?

8. REMEMBERING COMMUNITY IN DIFFICULT TIMES

Learn

One route to compassion for others is through solidarity in times of suffering. Solidarity means coming together in community, with feeling and purpose. When people are suffering and have a friend, relative, or group to be with or talk to, it helps reduce the pain.

Practice

Please think of a time you came together with a friend, relative, or group of people, and offered them your presence while they were suffering in pain.

What was going on for your friend or relative?	What did it feel like to you to listen to the story?	What did you do or say to your friend or relative?	How did they respond?	Would you do anything differently? If yes, what would You do differently?

Reflect

- Were you able to stay present, listen, and not share your thoughts?
- Did you get distracted and think of other things?
- What happened inside your body when you sat with your friend or relative in pain?

⑨ COURAGE AND BRAVERY

Learn

Self-compassion requires courage and bravery. Strength and a willingness to touch pain and suffering are the heart and soul of compassionate courage. Most people spend a lot of energy blocking out pain and suffering because they are afraid of it. Courage and bravery help teens face fear. Let's look at your levels of courage and bravery.

Practice

Here are some questions to promote courage and bravery:

Finish the following sentence.

I felt brave when. . .

_____

_____

_____

_____

What happened, and what did you do, when you were brave?

_____

_____

_____

_____

How afraid was I?

(Mark one number that corresponds to how afraid you felt. 0 is not afraid at all. 10 is the most afraid anyone could ever be.)

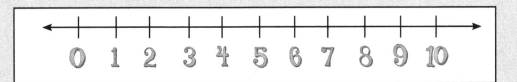

Where did I feel fear, bravery, and/or courage, in my body?

_____

_____

_____

_____

_____

What were the after effects of being brave?

(Check all that apply)

☐ Strengthened   ☐ Anxious

☐ Happy   ☐ Elated

☐ Sad   ☐ Tired and depleted

☐ Angry   ☐ Energized

☐ Agitated

Reflect

- When you're in pain, how brave do you feel?

- When you see someone suffering, do you feel empowered to help?

- Some people think being compassionate leads to being taken advantage of or as a sign of weakness. What do you think about this statement?

10A. DIFFERENTIATING BETWEEN SELF-EMPATHY, EMPATHY, AND SELF-COMPASSION

Learn

Empathy is the practice of getting curious about another person, for the purpose of appraising things, as they see/experience it, from their perspective. Appraising includes looking at the person's emotion and behavior, and tapping into your own internal information system beyond the senses. When we set the intention to be open, have balanced attention, and focus it on the other person, we practice empathizing with them. Conversely, self-empathy is an intentional practice of identifying experiences, needs, wants, desires, and wishes. It is the intentional application of open, balanced attention on oneself; getting curious about needs, wants, desires, wishes, dreams, etc. Activating self-empathy for the purpose of caring for oneself (including but not limited to identifying and being willing to act to relieve one's own suffering) allows people to arrive at relationships with more resources for serving others. Self-empathy, when practiced with the intention of connecting with others, is deeper than self-awareness, self-esteem, and narcissism. It's a manifestation of the metaphor of putting the oxygen mask on oneself before helping a child or dependent adult on an airplane with a depressurizing cabin. Practicing self-empathy involves setting an intention and focusing attention with a purpose. It strengthens the empathy muscle promoting accurate identification of authentic experiences/needs in others, and results in effective acts of compassion. Where empathy and self-empathy refer to the full range of human experiences, self-compassion and compassion are restricted to experiences related to suffering (Edwin Rutsch, Personal communication, December 10, 2015).

There are many different kinds of empathy:

Cognitive Empathy relies on memory, logic, inference, and deduction to decode another person's experience. For example, cognitive empathy is employed when a person sees his or her friend get a paper cut, and remembers what it is like to get a paper cut. The memory of getting the paper cut serves as the reference point for understanding the wincing faces of a friend who cut his or her finger.

Affective Empathy involves perceiving and interpreting physical or emotional sensations within to understand a friend's experience. Some people, synesthetes and empaths for example, literally feel the physical and/or emotional experiences of others. Synesthetes are sensitive to the physical and emotional sensations of others, as evidenced by the riveting story of Dr. Joel Salinas. Dr. Salinas, himself a synesthete and neurologist, directly experiences symptoms reported by his patients. His empathic accuracy is very high. Intuitive empaths (Orloff, 1996), however, predominantly experience the emotions of others. Dr. Orloff is a medical doctor and empath herself, and feels the emotions and experiences her patients bring to her. These two kinds of people represent extreme ends of the spectrum of empathic ability, however, most of us possess this capacity to varying degrees. Just like we can cultivate better focus and attention through mindful awareness and meditation practices, so too can empathic capacity deepen with practice.

Compassionate Empathy is another word for compassion. When cognitive and affective empathy are balanced in that "sweet spot," a person can be deeply moved by another person's situation and have adequate mental control to respond effectively. This is compassion or compassionate empathy, and it arises when people feel emotionally connected to another's experience, while also capable of using rational thinking to act and problem solve.

Functional Empathy is often seen in business, commerce, and production. Product designers, marketing and advertising professionals, as well as salespeople all use empathy as part of their work. They tune in to the needs, wants, desires, and challenges of their end user to create products consumers will buy. This kind of empathy is employed for the purpose of creating products for the consumer marketplace, and it is also the foundation of business psychology. Functional empathy has the intentional aim of serving needs of people who will ultimately be consumers in the marketplace; it serves a function. On an individual basis, functional empathy can also be defined as manipulation or the attunement toward others, for the purpose of meeting one's own goals. This type of empathy lacks the altruism associated with seeking to know the perspective of others, for no other reason than to know them more intimately.

Transactional Empathy is another unique form of empathy employed in the realm of business, and is restricted to helping professionals who accept a fee for their service.

Transformational Empathy is yet another kind of empathy with profound healing benefits. When practiced with attention to the ever unfolding moment-to-moment changes, it transforms individuals, communities, and systems. Transformational empathy is the authentic appraisal of another person's experience for no other reason than to understand that person. The agenda to sell or heal remains absent here, even though healing does occur.

Practice

The Spectrum of Empathy (Edwin Rutsch, Personal communication, December 31, 2015):

- Looking at the Spectrum of Empathy, try to find examples of the different kinds of empathy in your teen's life, and discuss them.
- If your teen can't find some examples, offer some that you may be aware of.
- Enjoy a discussion about the different types of empathy, as a means of opening your teen's mind to the kinds of empathy that feel good and deepen relationships versus empathy that is manipulative and other-serving.

Reflect

- What is it like to think about some types of empathy being helpful and healing, while others may not be?
- Did you ever encounter someone who seemed caring and kind, but something didn't quite feel right? When that happens, empathy may be at play for selfish reasons.
- Discuss the kinds of empathy your teen offers to others. Do they ever offer up good listening and tenderness with ulterior motives? When? Why?
- Reassure your teen that these various forms of empathy are all common and that there need not be shame around empathizing with ulterior motives, just mindful awareness, self-kindness, and shared humanity.

EMPATHY CIRCLE: REFLECTIVE LISTENING & SPEAKING

Learn

When training teens in self-compassion, listening to themselves and learning to be their own mirror is a critical and foundational skill. The Empathy Circle is a wonderful practice for cultivating these skills, and sourced in the work of Carl Rogers. Practiced in dyads, or small groups, Empathy Circles are highly effective in training teens to listen carefully to their own thoughts, filtering them, and decoding them with kindness and self-acceptance.

Practice

In a circle of three to four participants:

1. The first person selects whom they will speak to.
2. Then they speak about whatever comes up for them.
3. The listener reflects back whatever they've heard; paraphrasing and repeating the content as accurately as possible. This continues until the speaker feels heard to their satisfaction and states so: **"I feel heard."**
4. Next, the listener becomes the speaker, and selects another person from the group to speak to, and receive reflection back of what was said.

*This pattern continues back and forth for 2-6 minutes per speaker, or until they feel heard. Predetermine the time allotted to each speaker, and use a timer.

Speaker Tips

- Pause often to give the listener a chance to reflect what he or she heard.
- Remember that you are guiding the listener to hear you to your satisfaction. If the listener does not reflect accurately, please feel free to correct him or her until you feel heard and understood.

Active Listener

- Reflect back, summarize, paraphrase, etc., what you hear as best you can.
- There is no right and wrong. Don't worry about getting it perfect, the speaker will let you know how he or she wants to be heard and understood.
- While the speaker is talking, refrain from asking questions, judging, analyzing, detaching, diagnosing, advising, or sympathizing.
- Avoid sharing memories or experiences that come to mind.
- When it's your turn to speak, you can say anything you want.

Silent Listeners

- You can listen and be present with the empathic listening between the speaker and active listener.
- You will soon have a turn to actively listen and speak.

Modification

You can practice this exercise with just two people. You and your teen, or two teens, can empathically listen to one another in a back and forth pattern using the structure mentioned previously. It is very effective with just two people, too!

Reflect

- Was there a difference between listening for the sake of listening, and listening with the intention to repeat back what you've heard? What is your take on each? Are there benefits/drawbacks to each way of listening?
- What is it like to be listened to without the other person saying anything at all? How does it compare to a typical conversation, or even the one where your listener repeated your statements?
- What is it like to listen to other people, and not be welcome to speak up?
- Was it hard or easy to suppress your own thoughts while being the identified listener?
- Some people feel robotic when they paraphrase the speaker's statements. Did you feel that way?
- When receiving empathic listening, it can be surprising to hear how our thoughts come out of our mouths. Did anything surprise you, or leave you feeling uncomfortable, when you were actively listened to?

(11.) SETTING THE INTENTION TO LISTEN: A DAILY LISTENING PRACTICE

Learn

According to Mark Goulston, MD, author of *Just Listen* (2010), nobody listens, ever. He suggests we utilize quick judgments, or filters, to figure out whom and what we are listening to. The filters prevent us from being open and truly listening, restricting us to only hearing. Here are the first filters we most commonly use to evaluate what we are hearing:

- Gender
- Generation (age)
- Nationality
- Ethnicity
- Education level
- Emotion

The message here is think about what you hear, your thoughts, and then filter the words before they come out. The ideas that arise in the mind may seem compelling and true, but they aren't always accurate. Don't believe everything you think, especially when listening to others because one's own thoughts can interfere with the listening process. Let us not take our own thoughts about what others say too seriously.

Practice

- Today and every day, dedicate yourself to truly listen to others.

- Set aside your judgments, and all the stuff you already know.

- Set the intention to focus your attention on the other person and their words. It's okay if your own ideas come to mind and distract you; just return to listening with your open heart.

Reflect

- Did you listen wholeheartedly today?

- Did your mind wander when you listened? Did questions and comments come up that seemed very important to share?

- Were you able to suppress thoughts and reactions, stories and memories, while intentionally listening to someone else?

- Do you listen to you?

- Do you follow the words that come out of your mouth?

(12.) SELF-EMPATHY: THE LIGHT OF ATTENTION

Learn

Self-empathy is the practice of seeking to know oneself by intentionally engaging observing ego, as if looking inward from the outside, with curiosity, interest, open, balanced awareness, and above all else, acceptance. This practice enhances one's ability to "see" feeling states, creating a language and experience base to heal and use with others. Self-empathy is therefore the foundation of empathy, which is essential for identifying suffering, and also an integral part of compassion for self and other.

Self-empathy is not the same as introspection and self-awareness. There is a qualitative difference between looking in and noticing one is in pain, feeling good, or has a need vs. saying yes to a feeling or experience, embracing it, then surrounding it with acceptance and/or compassion (Erick Medina, Personal communication, September 6, 2014).

Practice

Imagine the lamp pictured here.

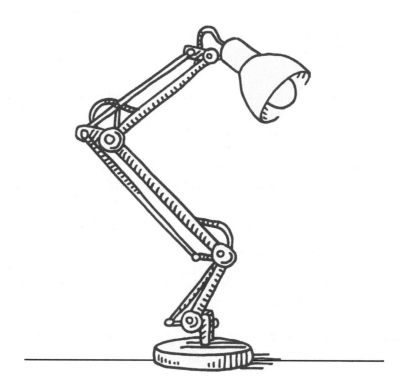

It's the same as the lamp in the Pixar short, *Luxo*, however, for our purposes, it has a magical extra dimension. It can bend inward like this:

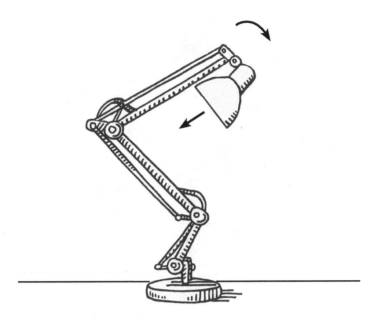

It is also a representation of you, me, or any one of us.

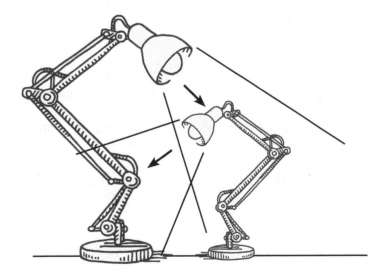

See how the neck of the lamp can move, reflecting the light in different directions?

Well, the lamp pictured here can send its light beam out, and redirect it back to itself, like a boomerang.

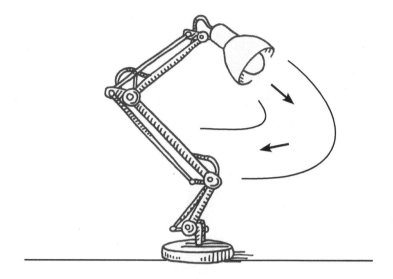

When you place your attention on yourself, with intentional and purposeful curiosity, you are practicing self-empathy.

- Imagine a yellow beam of light originating from either your heart, or your forehead at the bridge of your nose, and going outward to a spot of your choosing. The spot could be a tree, a photo, or a speck of dirt. Whatever you choose is perfect!

- Just look at this beam of light going from you to the spot, for a brief moment.

- The longer you keep your attention on the beam of light, the stronger your focus and concentration become. It also strengthens your ability to truly see what's going on inside you.

- Imagine the yellow beam of light bends at the spot, and now returns to you and pours into your heart space.

- Keep your attention on the beam of light. The longer your focus on it, and the more vivid it becomes in your mind, the stronger your mind and self-empathy skills become.

Reflect

- Discuss self-esteem and self-criticism.

- Explore the nature of ego, how it is ever changing as we grow, learn, and develop.

- Encourage teens to hold on to their own self-worth regardless of what is happening around them.

13. PRESCRIPTION OF PLAY

Learn

Play is one of the most self-compassionate practices people of any age can offer themselves. Human beings are so driven to play that they do so absent encouragement, toys, and even in times of political unrest. In 2015, I proposed a Prescription of Play! for healing Educational Trauma (Thomas et al, 2015) with the understanding that play has healing, educational, and developmental properties. In fact, the United Nations High Commission on Human Rights (1989) recognized play as a basic right of every child and adolescent. Ensuring that children of all ages retain this right is a fundamental way of promoting self-compassion practices in young people.

Play is optional. It is a special time when teens can freely join or leave, quit or continue, without any pressure to comply other than the desire to have fun (Gray, 2013). At a time when school pressures contribute to epidemic levels of stress, anxiety, depression, and suicidality, freedom to play holds tremendous value for child development. In the Romantic era of 1789–1848, Rousseau (in Rifkin, 2009) advised parents to let their children play, indulge in sports, pursue joy, thus elevating childhood to a higher status. When allowed to play, teens experience empathy and compassion, in their bodies and souls. When playing, they enter a state of *flow*, or optimal experience, where anxiety, depression, and worry momentarily fall away (Csikszentmihalyi, 1990; Gray, 2013). Since young people are being pressured with adult-like demands at younger and younger ages, encouraging them to play serves as a foundational way of helping them acquire self-compassion skills.

Practice

- Give teens verbal permission to play.

- Encourage play.

- Seek to know if teens play, how they play, how frequently, and what it is like for them when they play.

- Facilitate opportunities to play.

- Play with your teen.

Reflect

- What is it like to encourage play as an intervention and self-compassion practice?

- Some people equate play with frivolously wasting away time. What values do you hold about play?

- Would you give yourself permission to play? (Question for both the reader of this text, as well as for the teen in your life.)

SELF-CRITICISM DOES NOT PROMOTE SELF-ESTEEM

Learn

According to Chris Germer (2009), when we feel badly there is a sense that we do not deserve to feel better. This is not true. We deserve relief from suffering, and self-compassion practices are how we get there. Self-esteem is how we know we deserve care, kindness, love, and respect, however, it is fickle. Self-esteem depends on circumstances being just right for it to flourish. When self-compassion is cultivated, self-esteem rises and remains stable. Likewise, self-compassionate people tend to have higher levels of self-esteem that do not fluctuate when challenges, pain, suffering, and turmoil arise (Neff, 2011).

Teens need to bypass habitual patterns of criticizing, punishing, and isolating. Many believe harsher treatment yields better results, however, this perspective harms developing children. Teens who have internalized harsh parental voices and/or punitive super-egos may engage in higher levels of self-criticism. According to Germer, people tend to self-criticize, self-isolate, and become self-absorbed. Kristin Neff's (2011) three components of self-compassion offer teens ways of counteracting habitual patterns of responding to negative experiences with self-criticism. These three components are:

1. Self-kindness

2. Common humanity

3. Mindful awareness and balance in the face of negative experiences

Neff (2011) encourages her readers to see all people as composed of good and bad qualities, as those who make mistakes and also do great things. These positive and negative dimensions are aspects of being human common to all. Remembering this, especially in times of suffering, allows teens to preserve self-esteem when it might otherwise weaken with hardship. It simultaneously cultivates equanimity—the mental or emotional balance, especially needed in difficult situations.

Practice: Self-Criticism Begone!

Have teens answer the following questions. Then explore the reflection questions.

Reflect

• Discuss self-esteem and self-criticism.

• Explore the nature of ego, how it is ever changing as we grow, learn, and develop.

• Encourage teens to hold on to their own self-worth regardless of what is happening around them.

SELF-CRITICISM BEGONE!

I criticize myself when _____

_____

_____

_____ .

Self-esteem can be fickle and change depending on circumstances. Have you noticed times when you felt stronger, more capable, and competent? Have you noticed times when you felt proud to be you? Please write about one or two of these times:

_____

_____

_____

_____

_____

_____

Write about a time (or two) when you felt weak and not proud to be you? Did you criticize yourself? Did you think about your problems a lot? Were you open to being with others, or were you more closed and isolated?

_____

_____

_____

_____

_____

Some people think their internal negative self-talk helps them reach higher levels of performance, and get better at life. Have you ever felt that thinking negatively about yourself would help you in some way? If so, did it? Please write about this, and trust you will be releasing harmful patterns just by writing them down!

_____

_____

_____

_____

Self-Reminder: Thinking about a time when you were in pain, list all of the negative qualities that come to mind about yourself:

- _____

- _____

- _____

- _____

Then, next to each negative quality, list the opposite quality. Here's an example

Negative Quality		Opposite Quality
Useless	◄--►	Helpful
Hurtful	◄--►	Kind and caring
Mean	◄--►	Pleasant
Selfish	◄--►	Generous

Negative Quality		Opposite Quality
	◄--►	
	◄--►	
	◄--►	
	◄--►	

Truthfully, we all hold a mixture of these qualities in different proportions. Offsetting negative thinking with balance and common humanity in mind reduces suffering while contributing to healthy self-concept.

FORGIVENESS AND SELF-FORGIVENESS

Learn

Forgiveness doesn't accept and tolerate bad behavior. It understands that we are all human; we are imperfect and make mistakes. Forgiveness also leaves room for healthy boundaries and limits to be set when and wherever necessary, while also honoring common humanity in individuals who cause harm. Neff's (2009) research showed that self-compassionate people are more apt to forgive the transgressions of others. Forgiveness has a healing and soothing effect on the person who offers it and, therefore, serves as a foundational self-compassion practice.

When teens blame themselves for problems and mistakes, they engage the self-critical part of their ego. Instead, encouraging them to practice self-forgiveness relieves some suffering. One way to encourage teens to forgive themselves is to remind them that **we are all interconnected; we all make mistakes**. This wisdom relieves pressure, and prevents isolation, by freeing teens from feeling like all the world's problems are their fault. Because of the deeply interconnected nature of human life, teens are only partially responsible for their problems. Typically, problems arise when a number of unfortunate variables collide. Teens are rarely, if ever, the sole reason/cause of the problems in their lives, and deserve to be reminded of this so they can practice self-forgiveness when they mess up.

Tara Brach, PhD, (2012) clarifies that self-forgiveness is not a means of excusing the inner beast, and allowing it to rule. Rather self-forgiveness is a way of befriending the beast and trusting that it lives in everyone. When teens practice self-forgiveness, they open to their negative experiences with loving, kindness, and a warm heart. Promoting teens practicing self-forgiveness is one way for them to heal themselves while integrating the full range of human experience.

Practice

Have your teen fill out the following worksheet, then explore reflection questions.

Reflect

* The forgiveness/self-forgiveness inventory can be very challenging for people to complete. Trust that any fear, anger, discomfort, and resistance that emerges is being released as you feel it, and is also a natural effect of this practice.

* Accept yourself, with a kind, loving, warm, and open heart, if you are not yet ready to forgive.

* Invite teens to set the intention to be forgiving. This means that they have the willingness to forgive, yet do not require it of themselves before the time is just right.

FORGIVENESS AND SELF-FORGIVENESS

Things I hold against myself	Things I hold against others	Forgiveness granted (write yes or no)[1]

---

[1] It is okay to not be ready to forgive. Just be open to reexamining this over time.

(16.) DIFFERENTIATING SELF-EMPATHY, EMPATHY, AND COMPASSION

Learn

Empathy is when we seek to know the full experience of another person (good, bad, ugly, happy, sad, etc.). Self-empathy arises when we intentionally look inward, with deeper attention and focus than self-awareness, to know our own full experience. Both of these differ from compassion, which first relies on being empathic and interested in someone's experience (yours or others'), and ends with learning that the other person is suffering.

Practice

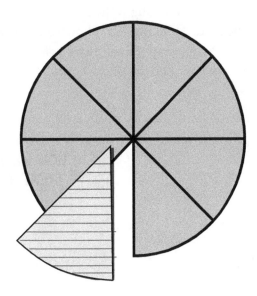

- Looking at the pie, please think of it as the full range of human experience.

- Each slice of pie represents a different emotional, physical, or sensory experience (i.e., joy, sadness, pain, anger, fear, injury, dizziness, nausea, worry, peace, etc.).

- The striped piece of pie represents any and all types of suffering. It stands out in a different texture because it is also called compassion.

- All the other slices of human experience are those we see when we practice empathy.

- Compassion (or self-compassion) is one aspect of empathy (or self-empathy), where the latter refers to the whole universe of potential human experiences, and the former focuses only on suffering.

Reflect

- People frequently use empathy and compassion interchangeably. Sometimes they even mean kindness and respect, something warm and fuzzy, which isn't quite the same as empathy or compassion. Do you see a difference between the two?

17. BE YOUR OWN BEST FRIEND!

Learn

One of the essentials of self-compassion is self-kindness; teens offering themselves the kind of regard and consideration they would their very best friend. Every time teens treat themselves kindly and with special regard, they tell others and the universe that they embrace their inherent worthiness. Doing so even when it is hard to believe rewires the brain so that feeling inherently worthy becomes reality.

Practice

How well do you treat yourself? Looking at the empty graph below, and think about someone who is your dear friend or beloved. Thinking about how you treat yourself compared to your friend in the three categories listed on the graph, draw a star or a bar to identify whether you treat yourself better, same, or worse than your dear friend.

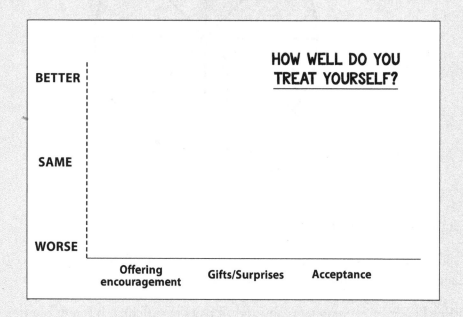

Reflect

• When negative thoughts arise, instead of following that train of thought, prompt your teen to ask themselves what their perfect best friend would say in this situation. Just thinking about this strengthens self-kindness connections in the brain.

2

Interpersonal Neurobiology of Self-Compassion and Teens

We'll explore the science of self-compassion in this chapter, with special emphasis on the interpersonal neurobiology of developing teens (Siegel, 2013). Self-compassion is associated with reduced negative thinking, less fear and isolation, and less negative self-judgment. It is also associated with increased happiness, thriving, flourishing, and the ability to hold good and bad together, at the same moment. Studies show that self-compassionate people are less anxious and depressed, which implores adult caregivers to share it with the teens in your life. We'll consider the effects of self-compassion on the amygdala, concentration, relationships, as well as launching, and individuating in this chapter. This chapter also includes activities and practices that impart research findings.

The following exercises will provide research on the mindful awareness component of self-compassion for teens.

(1.) GENTLE BREATH PRACTICE

Learn

Meditation and mindful awareness practices are evidence-based methods of increasing self-awareness, the capacity to be aware of awareness, and executive functioning. Tuning inward and setting the intention to stay present in the moment, with kindness and compassion to oneself is one way of increasing attention. Just a few minutes of mindful attention to breath several times every day improves well-being. Doing so promotes a certain awareness of kindness that arises when we honor each other with undivided attention. Here is a breath practice combined with kindness to self.

Practice

- Offer instructions for a basic breath meditation, as in **25 Breaths** (Chapter 1), or any other that you, or your teen, prefer.

- Set the intention to sit or walk with attention focused on the in-and-out flow of air through the nostrils, filling the lungs and belly before leaving through the nostrils again.

- When attention wanders away from the breath, notice, and silently say to yourself:

  "It's okay, everyone's mind wanders. I'll refocus my attention on my breath."

- Offer encouragement to your teen to speak gently and kindly to him- or herself when silently saying this phrase.

Reflect

- This dual purpose practice increases mindful awareness capacity, while cultivating kindness toward self. Gently reminding teens to be as tender with themselves as they would be with a young child is a way to train in kindness, with this breath practice.

- Is there any self-talk or beliefs that get activated? If so, what are they?

- Discuss how to utilize gentle and soothing self-talk when teens find themselves in tricky situations.

- Processing the experience of this practice opens the gateway to explore failure, and how to respond to it with self-compassion.

  FAIL is an acronym for <u>F</u>irst <u>A</u>ttempt <u>I</u>n <u>L</u>earning.

- When teens are empowered to see their failures as moments of learning and acquiring new skills/ information/abilities, it becomes an act of self-compassion. This type of empowerment is also an antidote to harmful educational practices that rank and punish students who don't perform adequately.

2. MORE THAN CHORES: A WORK MEDITATION

Learn

Research shows that consistent mindful awareness practices are a component in building self-compassion (Neff, 2011) as well as other critical components of adolescent development. Work Meditation honors the Zen intention to be fully present for all moments. It trains teens in directing their attention to the task at hand, when the task involves mundane, repetitive motions.

Chores can be dull and disengaging, creating conflict between teens and parents. The benefit of daily and weekly chores in a teen's life cannot be overstated here. It is essential to healthy emancipation into adulthood, and also an opportunity for teens to be an active part of a community. When chores are carried out as a Work Meditation, they also serve to promote mindful awareness and interconnection, two components of self-compassion (Neff, 2011).

Practice

- Empower parents to assign chores to teens with consistency.

- Discuss:

    - "Chores may be boring and crummy. Many people dislike chores; some find comfort in them. What are chores like for you?"

    - "Since you need to participate in the mini community that is your family, let's make it an activity that also trains your brain and heals your heart."

    - "Whenever you are doing a chore, think only about the activity you are engaged in. Notice your body, how it moves while you do the chore. Tune in to any feelings that may arise as you complete your chores."

    - "Allow the feelings and thoughts to be honored as they come to mind. Try to let them go once they've been acknowledged. Your mind may really want to stay on a topic that arises, like how boring the chores are, see if you can let it go."

    - "When you notice your attention wandering away from the chore, gently bring your attention back. That's where the magic happens. Every time you notice you are not paying attention, and decide to bring your attention back to the chore at hand, you are strengthening your mind. When it happens with loving kindness, it also heals the heart."

Reflect

- Did the addition of the Work Meditation to chores effect your teen's perspective on chores? Did your teen's opinion of chores change? Improve/worsen?

- Invite teens to ponder questions like:

    - How might we find peace while doing things we don't like? (Self-compassion in teens grows exponentially when they can hold this kind of question without needing to receive an answer. The capacity to hold a question invites unique answers and promotes patience.)

3. TEENS AND MUSIC: SELF-COMPASSION THROUGH THE EAR

Learn

The sacculus is a tiny part of the inner ear, once thought to be functionless, first identified by Barry Blesser, scholar and author. In his 2009 paper, "The Seductive (Yet Destructive) Appeal of Loud Music," he reframed the concern about how loud music was affecting developing ears in children to a question of why they do it to begin with. His research suggests that loud music activates the sacculus, which triggers pleasure centers in the hypothalamus. In fact, Blesser reported that the brain releases endorphins in response to the loud music. More exposure to loud music also tends to promote increased desire for loud music. There is a circular reaction between loud music, the sacculus, and the experience of pleasure through endorphins being released in the brain. Blesser discovered that music played at a volume over 90 decibels causes the sacculus to react in a "self-stimulatory" fashion.

Practice

- With your teen, find three to five samples of music that range from your teen's preferred tracks and artists, to the kinds you like. Add in a few samples of music that neither of you prefer, and seek a wide range of influences and origins of music in the samples chosen.

- No music ability is required for this practice.

- Along with your teen, listen to each music selection and fill in the following practice sheet.

Reflect

- Discuss the impact music has on your teen. What is their unique relationship to music? Some teens have strong attachments, others can take it or leave it. Exploring this will help you determine if this practice is right for your teen.

- Discuss this statement with your teen:

Music is the language of the heart.

- There are musical genres specifically designed to promote healing. Explore these types of music, and see if any interest your teen.

- Honoring teens' use of loud music as a means of coping with pain is a sign of compassion. It is not necessary to condone and praise the behavior as it can damage the inner ear, however, it benefits long-term healing when the behavior is understood with loving allowance. This becomes the bridge for addressing the concern, with your teen, in a collaborative way.

- This activity does not require repetition to be effective. As a one-time only practice, it introduces teens to the healing and self-compassionate aspects of music, essentially planting the seed for future deeper exploration, if desired.

SELF–COMPASSION THROUGH MUSIC

	Music selection 1	Music selection 2	Music selection 3	Music selection 4	Music selection 5
How loud was the music sample?					
How do you feel when you listen to this music sample?					
Do you feel the music anywhere in your body? If so, where? Record what it feels like? (Positive/ Negative sensations, such as: tingly, tense, invigorating, like lightning going through your body, etc.)					
Explore themes in lyrics or musical instruments that are noteworthy or impactful to teens.					

4. HOW IS MY AMYGDALA TODAY?

Learn

The amygdala is the "reptilian" part of the brain that detects danger. It can get pretty sensitive when people get stressed out, hungry, tired, or even excited and leveling up in a game. When you get to know the ways amygdalae can get overactive, you can literally use your mind to calm it down, or wake it up!

Practice

Read the following to the teen in your life:

- Sit comfortably, or lie down. Select a position that is comfortable for you.

- Take three deep breaths all the way into your belly.

- Follow the air as it enters your nostrils, as it travels into your lungs, and fills them before moving to your belly.

- Notice the air as it moves out of your belly, up through your lungs, and out through your mouth.

After three deep breaths, begin to imagine your brain, see it in your mind's eye:

- Imagine the lower part of the brain that sits at the base, connecting to your neck. It's the "reptilian" part, the oldest part of us that remembers how to survive in the wild, and still thinks we need protection from beasts.

- Imagine the central part of your brain, it's kind of like the heart of the brain because it is right there in the middle and it is also where our emotions arise and subside. This middle "mammalian" brain is responsible for feelings of sadness, anger, grief, joy, and more.

- The third part of the brain is like a thick carpet covering the central middle "mammalian" brain. It is called the "upstairs" brain or the "primate" brain because it's where our most sophisticated thinking takes place. It differentiates people from animals.

- Now that you can imagine your brain in three parts, and understand them, you've just succeeded in getting curious and familiar with yourself! Congratulations!

With the three brain parts in mind, we are now going to focus on the "upstairs" brain and the "reptilian" brain.

- The amygdala responds to threats of danger, even if they are only imaginary.

- You can use your "upstairs" brain to calm your amygdala by focusing on these parts of the brain when you are in a calm state.

- Imagine two little peas deep in the central bottom area of your brain behind your eyes.

- Now, ask your little amygdalae:

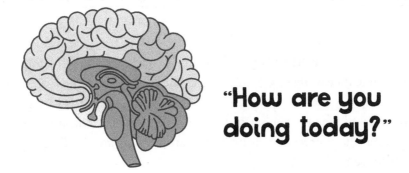

"How are you doing today?"

- Try to stay open to the possibility that your amygdala can tell you how it is. The first thing that comes to mind is the truth, if you believe so.

- Sit with your amygdala in your mind's eye. And just allow yourself to know that part of your mind and body.

- Shift your attention to your "upstairs" brain. Thank it for being logical and rational when amygdala freaks out.

(Terms taken from Goulston, 2010; Siegel & Payne Bryson, 2011.)

Reflect

- Help teens understand that by visiting with the amygdala and "upstairs" brain in a quiet space, they can get to know them better. Doing so helps gain control of amygdala when/if it freaks out unnecessarily.

- When teens know the parts of themselves that determine emotional reactions, they can tenderly hold these reactions, and offer loving kindness to their brain if it acts like a reptile in danger.

- Tell teens to check in with the amygdala. Say hi when calm and quiet. It's a new and different way of relating to oneself, and it's how we level up as conscious human beings.

⑤ EFFECTS OF SELF-KINDNESS ON THE BRAIN

Learn

According to Kristin Neff (2011), self-kindness activates the left temporal pole and insula in the brain, while increasing oxytocin. An increase in this hormone is associated with trust, safety, calm, connection, generosity, warmth, and self-compassion. It is very powerful as it is the same hormone released when a mother nurses her baby. When teens are encouraged to practice self-kindness, even the slightest bit, it promotes attachment and healing, while offsetting amygdala hijack and/or self-criticism.

Practice: Spending Time with Me

Think of all the things you like to do. Some may involve others, some may occur alone. For this practice, think only about those activities you can do alone that bring happiness. List at least ten things you can do to feel happy, calm, content, and/or cared for:

1. _____

2. _____

3. _____

4. _____

5. _____

6. _____

7. _____

8. _____

9. _____

10. _____

- When the list is complete, set it aside for a brief moment.

- Close your eyes (if comfortable, otherwise cast your gaze downward and focus on a spot of your choosing).

- Take a deep breath, noticing the air travel all the way down into your belly, inflating it. Exhale slowly.

- Open your eyes.

- Reread the list, being open to the possibility that one item on your list will pop out, and appeal for any reason.

- No need to think about it, just do that one activity on your list that makes you happy. Do it for one minute, at least, or as long as you like.

- Every day, set aside time to do something you like, even if only for a very brief while.

- Doing something you like is an act of self-kindness. It primes the brain to respond in ways that are caring to you.

Reflect

- What was it like to think of things you like to do alone? Easy or hard? Did a lot or very little come to mind?

- You should see your leisure time as time well spent. Teens need breaks between school, work, family, sports, tutoring, and volunteering. Taking time out to play in whatever way feels free and inspiring promotes self-kindness, self-compassion, and passion.

- How might you be your very best friend and give yourself permission to spend time in ways that nurture you?

6. GRATITUDE AND HAPPINESS: SELF-COMPASSION SAYS YES TO HAPPINESS

Learn

According to Martin Seligman et al. (2005), the practice of gratitude results in research subjects experiencing instant increases in happiness scores. Keeping a consistent formal gratitude practice promotes more positive emotions, an ability to enjoy positive experiences, good health, resilience, and good relationships. The wish to be happy and free from harm is universal; everyone wants it. Practicing gratitude connects people to one another, infusing common humanity connection with the loving kindness components of self-compassion (Neff, 2011). When teens are encouraged to practice gratitude *and* pursue happiness, it carves out space for healing and relief from suffering. There are many ways to encourage happiness, and formal gratitude practices are one way.

Practice

- Keep a gratitude journal.

- Every day write down three things you are grateful for.

- Try to write different things on different days, without too much repetition.

- If you need to repeat things you are grateful for, know it is okay to do so.

- Think about the things you may take for granted, and write them down. Shelter, food, and clothing are basic necessities that when met create happiness, and when not met, they create suffering.

- By focusing on the things you have, and are grateful for, you create pathways of happiness in your brain. These pathways of happiness counteract pain and suffering.

Reflect

- What is it like for you to practice gratitude?

- Do you have a lot or a little to be grateful for?

- Does it ever feel pointless? Many people question the power of mindful awareness practices because they are so simple. It is very challenging to focus on simple things and trust in their power. When you do so, it strengthens your own inner power. Inner power is associated with both happiness and self-compassion.

7. THE MIRROR NEURON SYSTEM AND SELF-COMPASSION

Learn

Our brains are hardwired to create a representation of other people's physical, emotional, and sensory experiences. When Adam feels a cut in his finger, or heartache over a breakup, his friend Amanda may sense either the finger pain, or the heartache, vicariously, or not at all. When this occurs, the system that is active is called the *mirror neuron system*, and it relates to self-compassion because some of our suffering is our mirror neuron systems telling us about the suffering of others.

When teens live in families with stress, worry, anxiety, depression, grief, and/or illness, some of the stress they encounter can be like "catching germs" in the air. Instead of catching a cold, these "germs" can cause suffering. For example, parents stressed about work, relationships, finances, and more may not tell their teens the nature of their problems yet still transmit the stress and negative experience through the mirror neuron system. In another example, teens offering comfort to a friend may encounter "emotional contagion"—experiencing their friends' painful feelings. This is a form of empathy, and it causes suffering when healthy ego boundaries are not in place. This is not the only cause of teen suffering, nor is it always present, just one dimension. It also explains common humanity and the universal nature of suffering in neurological terms. Educating teens about the mirror neuron system removes a great deal of stigma and responsibility from teens already struggling with intense emotions common to their phase of development. By sharing this type of information with teens, it also promotes individuation and healthy personality development.

Practice I: Teach About the Mirror Neuron System

- Describe and discuss the mirror neuron system with your teen.

Practice II: "Is This Mine?"

When teens find themselves in distress, in certain instances it can be very important to identify whose distress they are feeling.

- In moments of distress, when nothing seems clear, ask yourself silently:

  "To whom does this feeling belong?"

- Remain open to whatever answer to your question arises.

- It's okay if an answer doesn't arise. That too is useful information. Perhaps more time is needed, and perhaps the feeling belongs to someone you don't know.

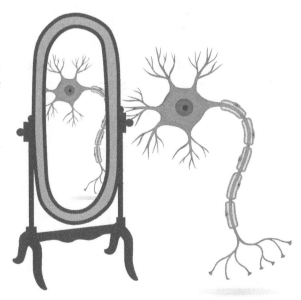

Reflect

- All teens go through a transition from childhood to adulthood. The pathway of development starts with a warm and responsive relationship with the caregiver, and results in launching and individuation around 18 to 21 years of age. In other words, teens need help becoming aware of, and getting through, the emancipation process. Life entails shifting and changing attachments and linkage with parents, guardians, relatives, and caregivers. Since these relations are grounded in the mirror neuron system, it can take time to reprogram for launching into independent adulthood.

- Discuss themes of: individuation, self-other differentiation, and how suffering can result from our interconnectedness with others. Reference the mirror neuron system to anchor the dialogue in concrete science terms.

Modification

Giftedness is associated with five overexcitabilities (Dabrowski, 1964):

    a. Psychomotor

    b. Imaginal

    c. Sensual

    d. Intellectual

    e. Emotional

The fifth overexcitability is highly correlated with being a prodigy, which may also include a hypersensitive mirror neuron system. This information is important for gifted teens because comorbidity with affective disorders is extremely prevalent. Every one of us has the potential to be great in some area. When that area involves emotional intelligence, the risk of pathologizing suffering runs very high. Profoundly gifted emotionally intelligent teens may need extra help learning whose experiences they are perceiving when they suffer.

3 Self-Compassion for Teens: No Longer a Child, Not Yet an Adult

Special considerations exist when using mindfulness and self-compassion practices with adolescents, specifically because they are transitioning from childhood to adulthood. Self-compassion practices designed with teens in mind cover the following four areas:

1. **Self-regulation**

   - This is the ability to respond to stress effectively, and return to a balanced state.

   - Problems with self-regulation manifest in teens as either hyperactivity or under arousal.

   - It can also arise as sound, light, tactile, and taste sensitivities.

   - Since learning requires students to be in a calm, alert state, the amount of energy required to self-regulate can detract from learning, compounding problems when ready states are hard to come by.

   - Stress can be both positive and negative; self-regulation helps teens manage both emotions.

   - Self-regulation minimizes sensation-seeking behaviors and/or peer pressures.

2. **Peer group membership and influence vs. tuning in to self**

   - Common humanity inspired by community service.

   - Internal motivation and power vs. extrinsic motivation and power.

   - Being tough as a means of being part of the group vs. the strength that comes from ongoing self-compassion practice.

3. **Launching:** The ups and downs of transitioning from childhood to adulthood

   - Exploring the difference between being vulnerability in childhood vs. vulnerability in adulthood.

   - Identifying the ways teens remain childlike, while also being adultlike.

   - Moving from dependency to interdependence.

4. **Creativity:** A key component of healthy development

   - Preserve and create opportunities for teens to be creative.

   - Any form of creativity stimulates healing and is therefore compassionate.

   - Offer vision board activities, collages, art, writing, drama, music, improv, dance, tinkering, robotics, coding, etc.

1. SELF-REGULATION PRACTICE 1: HUG ME

Learn

Self-regulation is the ability to process stressors and return oneself to a calm, alert, and balanced state. When a person does this, they are essentially practicing self-compassion by resetting the nervous system to a homeostatic point that does not support suffering. Having control over your nervous system so that you can shift yourself out of a suffering state is how self-regulation practices promote self-compassion. In this "Hug Me" practice, self-hugging releases the same hormones and chemicals as getting a hug from someone else.

Practice

- Reach both arms around yourself, grasping opposite shoulders with each hand.

- Hug yourself whenever you feel unsettled, worried, nervous, afraid, sad, or simply not yourself.

- The more you hug yourself, the more effective the practice becomes.

- Hugging yourself becomes more and more soothing the more you use it!

Reflect

- When your teen is stressed out, does a hug help?

- Some people don't like to be hugged when they are suffering. This is just another natural response. See if your teen likes to hug him- or herself instead of receiving a hug from someone else. If your teen doesn't like it either, it's okay. Some practices will resonate, some won't; choose only those that fit with your teen's unique design.

②. SELF-REGULATION PRACTICE 2: BODY SCAN WITH GROUNDING

Learn

Grounding (and centering) are synonymous with applying effort to self-regulate. When one is in a self-regulated state, one is grounded, or centered. Grounding practices tap into the collective wisdom source empowering people with energy and willpower when most needed. Quickly getting centered is a very self-compassionate practice when suffering sets in. The following practice has two parts: grounding and embodiment.

First, the grounding component of this practice promotes teens cultivating imagination properties associated with letting go. Releasing is a natural part of metabolism, health, healing, and recovery. The body naturally releases waste and toxins; grounding practices cultivate mind properties associated with releasing and letting go. According to the Buddha, a source of suffering is our attachment to and striving for sensual satisfaction. Freedom from suffering arises when we let go of this attachment, and stop grasping at it. Training teens in how to let go, even if only at the level of imagination, is a starting point for reducing suffering, and therefore also a self-compassion practice.

Second, the body scan practice promotes embodiment. Cognitive embodiment embraces the role of the body in cognition. Our experiences and emotions are directly related to movements, postures, and structures of the body, as well as events that arise in the body. For example, sleeping in an awkward position causes muscle strain and pain. Physical pain causes emotional suffering, the body is connected to the mental component of suffering. Connecting to one's body offers rich insight into the role our feelings and history have in health and disease, and can mitigate suffering. Self-compassion practices are those that foster health and well-being, and shift attention away from those that lead to suffering.

Practice

- Take three deep breaths all the way into your belly.

- Follow the air as it enters your nose, and travels through your lungs filling your belly.

- When you feel present in your body, imagine a connector that resides between your legs, where they meet your torso, around your tailbone.

- Imagine a cord. Notice its thickness, color, and the width.

- In your mind, connect this cord to yourself between your legs, at your tailbone. Once the cord is connected in your imagination, notice it drop down to the center of the earth. This happens instantaneously through your imagination.

- See the grounding cord connect to the ball of live energy that exists at the core of the earth.

- You are now hooked into Mother Earth's power grid, and She is supporting you with love and sustenance.

- Imagine all the negative and foreign energies you don't need flushing down your grounding cord.

- This is how you release energy you no longer need, and also access nourishing energy from the center of the earth.

- Now that you are solidly connected to the earth, check in with your body—starting at the top of your head, and moving down to your forehead, eyes, cheeks, and ears.

- While you scan these parts of your face and head, notice any tightness, tension, or tingling sensations. They may be pleasurable or uncomfortable sensations—just notice them. You don't have to do anything about it.

- Continue scanning your neck (back and front), as well as your shoulders, chest, and upper back. If you encounter any tightness or tension that bothers you, just say relax to that part of your body.

- You may also breathe in and out wherever there is tension. The air flow will melt it away if you patiently direct your attention and breath there long enough.

- Scan your abdomen, your middle and lower back, as well as your bottom.

- Shift your attention to the front of your body, and scan your legs, knees, and feet before checking the back of your legs and thighs, too.

Reflect

- What is it like to imagine connecting a grounding cord to your body, in your imagination?

- When we let go of things that don't serve us, we are making an effort to reduce suffering, leaving "letting go" as an act of self-compassion.

③ SELF-REGULATION PRACTICE 3: HEART TAP

Learn

Every now and then something happens and really rocks the ground we stand on. For those moments, turning to a trusted friend, relative, or therapist for support is helpful. In those moments when teens are alone, they can self-soothe in very intense moments with this simple practice that calms the nervous system.

Practice

- Tap your breastbone, in the center of your chest, with your fingertips.

- Tap as hard or as softly as you like.

- Tap as fast or as slow as is comfortable for you.

Reflect

- Though so very simple, this practice becomes more robust and more effective with consistent, repeated, and frequent use.

- This practice can be used in moments of distress, and need not be practiced only in calm moments for the effects to build.

Modification

- Adding the gentle command: "**I love you,**" signals to the brain and soul that you are worthy and deserving of love. This is an act of self-kindness in the face of suffering.

- It's okay for teens to say "**I love you**" to themselves even if they don't believe it. Silently uttering the words is enough to activate subtle changes. The more often subtle changes are activated, the larger the impact becomes.

- Feeling (and/or hearing about being) loved offsets suffering, even in moments when we feel utterly alone and disconnected from others.

4. SELF-REGULATION PRACTICE 4: 20 MINUTES OF AEROBIC ACTIVITY

Learn

Research shows that 20 minutes of aerobic activity sets brain activity in a calm, alert state. Students who spend energy on self-regulation may be sacrificing resources needed for learning. Physical activity, therefore, directs teens' energy where needed for optimal learning. It is self-compassionate to understand what one needs in order to operate at peak levels of performance. Short intervals of movement have profound effects on the developing brain, and upon learning outcomes. When a school in Fort Worth, Texas, increased recess to four times a day, for 15 minutes, they noticed happier students who were more successful in school.

Practice

- Take 20 minutes to move your body

- Do anything that gets your heart moving

  - Walk uphill
  - Run
  - Ride a bike
  - Skateboard really fast

Reflect

- Do you like to move your body? Why, or why not?

- Try an experiment:

  - On day 1, do your homework after 20 minutes of exercise.
  - On day 2, do your homework without exercising first.
  - Log your observations on the following below.

	Day 1	Day 2
How was your attention and concentration?		
How was your energy level? Were you tired or energized afterward?		
How did your homework flow? Smoothly to completion? Needing breaks?		

(5.) SELF-REGULATION PRACTICE 5: PLANNING

Learn

Planning out the day ahead with special attention to meals, rest, play, responsibilities, and deadlines is one way to increase self-regulation and live with self-compassion. Adequate food, nutrition, recreation, and sleep are essential to learning, growing, and self-regulating. When you set a plan for your day, understand it may change. Surprises occur and plans change, which may throw a wrench into your well-planned day. Flowing with these changes and a lighthearted approach reduce stress and maintain self-regulation. Both are self-compassionate ways of living.

Practice

Focus on your sleeping habits.

- Do you get enough sleep? Most students need 2 more hours of sleep than they regularly get.
- Is it possible to schedule your bedtime at the outset of your day to ensure you get enough sleep?
- Do you find yourself needing a nap after school?
- Do you sleep late on the weekend?

Pay attention to your need for food.

- When are you hungry?
- When are you able to make food for yourself, and eat it?
- Do you eat at regular intervals?

Consider play and recreation.

- Do you move your body in a fun way?
- Do you prioritize your time around getting outdoors and doing fun things?
- Can you add this to your daily routine, trusting it will bring health, happiness, and vitality?

Thinking about your chores and school assignments.

- Do you have enough time to work on them?
- Is it possible to schedule time in your day when you will be most alert and able to complete chores and assignments?
- Scheduling them into your day may seem mundane, however, it is one way to make sure things happen in a self-compassionate way.

Reflect

- Using the schedule that follows, fill in the times of day when you will eat/prepare food, rest or sleep, play, complete homework, and do your chores.

- Use the boxes to enter what you will eat, how you may play, and which assignments or chores you'll work on.

PLANNING

Time:	Meals/Food	Rest/Sleep	Play	School Assignments	Chores and Responsibilities
6:00 am					
7:00 am					
8:00 am					
9:00 am					
10:00 am					
11:00 am					
12:00 pm					
1:00 pm					
2:00 pm					
3:00 pm					
4:00 pm					
5:00 pm					
6:00 pm					
7:00 pm					
8:00 pm					
9:00 pm					
10:00 pm					
11:00 pm					
12:00 am					

(6.) SELF-REGULATION PRACTICE 6: SENSORY SENSITIVITIES

Learn

According to A. Jean Ayres (2005), sensory integration is how people make sense of, and use, information about their bodies and the environment around them. When the nervous system organizes this information well, teens are self-regulated. When sensory information is either over- or underwhelming, teens can expend excessive amounts of energy trying to cope. Since sensory integration is an unconscious phenomenon, gaining awareness of the effects allows teens to respond to situations in self-compassionate ways. Moreover, sensory integration forms the basis for learning and relating.

The following practice is an inventory to help teens discover if they have sensory sensitivities. Self-empathy about sensory sensitivities is essential for self-regulation, and ultimately a self-compassion practice.

Practice

Fill in the worksheet that follows by thinking about one sensory system at a time. For each one, think about the activities, sensations, and experiences that activate that system. For example, hiking activates the motor skills and planning system. Do you like/dislike it? Does it calm/soothe you, or agitate and arouse? For the tactile system, think about fabrics, textures, and objects that you like/dislike and that soothe/agitate. List the various fabrics, textures, or objects in each column according to your preferences. For interoception, explore the inner body and its sensations. Mind refers to mental activity, thoughts, beliefs, and memories, for example. And finally, relatedness is the sense of being aware of relationships with others.

Modification

- Parents, educators, and teachers can set up sensory stations for groups of teens to explore.

- Teens can walk through the rotations in smaller groups or individually, and use the worksheet mentioned previously to rate the different experiences.

- Examples of stations include:

   a. Jars of food, chemicals, organic matter to be used for smelling (keep the jars closed to preserve the scent, and include one of whole coffee beans to cleanse the nasal palate between smelling samples).

   b. Visually appealing and straining images, such as: vistas, horizons, kaleidoscope views, eye teasers, moving eye illusions, color blindness tests, 3-D images.

   c. A tactile station can be assembled using foods and substances commonly found in homes, schools, and clinic offices. Some examples include: a bowl of cold spaghetti noodles, a bag of Jell-O, a container of beans. Offer teens a blindfold and invite them to explore the different samples using hands only.

   d. Audio samples can include white noise, different forms of music, chanting, and prayer.

e. Offer teens a station with food they can taste. Include those that are familiar to their culture, as well as those that are foreign.

f. Motor planning opportunities can be combined with movement, vestibular, and proprioceptive opportunities by creating obstacle courses. Obstacle courses are a fun and creative way for teens to move their bodies. If you can let your teen create the course, it's an even better opportunity to practice motor planning and executive functioning.

Reflect

- The sensory system extends beyond the five senses we frequently think of.

- Exploring likes and dislikes in regard to the seven different systems helps teens know themselves more intimately.

- These likes and dislikes can be comforting during challenging moments, or elicit very strong reactions—both of which are important ways of knowing and caring for oneself.

SENSORY ACTIVITIES LOG

Sensory System	Likes	Dislikes	Soothing	Agitating
Movement (vestibular system)				
Position in space: Proprioception				
Motor skills and planning				
Touch				
Visual perception				
Auditory and language processing				
Smell				
Taste				
Interoception				
Mind				
Relatedness				

(7.) PEER GROUP VS. SELF–PRACTICE 1: MY FRIENDS, MY SELF

Learn

Peer group membership and influence can have a powerful effect on teens. Turning inward to heal wounds, and reduce suffering, may sound weird and off, when joining friends would be way more fun.

To balance this, honor the role your friends play in your life, and reflect upon the ways they support you. Your friends are already your posse of shared humanity, and at the same time, you contain an infinite wellspring of wisdom within you too. Taking the time to tap into that wellspring within leaves you a better friend and a healthier person.

Practice

In the chart below, for each prompt write an example that happens with your friends, and an example that happens when you're alone.

	My friends	My self
How do I find comfort with...		
What do I like to do with...		
Where do I like to spend time with...		
What times of days do I prefer to be with...		
How are parents different sources of comfort than...		
How are teachers different sources of comfort than...		
How are therapists different sources of comfort than...		

Reflect

Taking time to notice the differences in comfort offered by different people, including teens themselves improves one's ability to offer self-compassion.

(8.) PEER GROUP VS. SELF-PRACTICE 2: COMMON HUMANITY

Learn

Community service has become a component of many teens' educational programming. Unfortunately, it is devoid of meaning for many, and just another requirement to meet as they earn their high school diploma. Highlighting the interconnectedness of all beings and examining how serving others benefits teens reframes volunteering as an act of good that benefits them and their community.

His Holiness the fourteenth Dalai Lama said, "Our ancient experience confirms at every point that everything is linked together, everything is inseparable." When teens volunteer in their community, and choose a population or organization that is meaningful to them, the service has the potential to nurture their souls.

Practice

- Explain the interconnectedness of life to teens.

- Use the Internet as an example of how very interconnected we are.

- The Internet is also a good image representing the brain. Our brains are microrepresentations of the World Wide Web, meaning we have infinite potential to learn, create, and grow and connect.

- Help your teen see that the web is also a macrorepresentation of their community. When teens volunteer at an organization that resonates with their values and interests, it feeds their brains, grows dendrites and axonal connections, while also sustaining others.

- Even a little bit of volunteer work that is meaningful to teens themselves builds positive connections in the community, serves people teens may never know, and most importantly creates new connections in teen brains.

- These new brain connections promote health and well-being at both the micro (individual) and macro (community) levels.

Reflect

- Ask your teen to share desires, values, and interests. You may already know this from being in a relationship with your teen, however, it deepens the connection to ask again. What types of charitable organizations relate to them? List the values, desires, concerns, and interests here:

  - What do you care about? (ie: people, animals, climate, religion, politics, etc. . .)

  - What social issues concern you? (ie: human trafficking, lack of clean running water in developing countries, the wage gap, drug war, etc. . .)

  - Are there any charities that you strongly support? (ie: Red Cross, American Society for the Prevention of Cruelty to Animals, Unicef, etc. . .) If so, list them.

  - Do you have any concerns about your identity, race, ethnicity, religion, gender, or sexuality that are represented by a charity? If so, list the charity and concerns.

- What major issues in your community do you feel deserve attention? (ie: crime, access to parks, recreation, and wholesome food. . .)

- The power of the community service practice lies in connecting teens with others, and is amplified when expressly verbalized. Discussing the extent of impact their service has upon unknown others can be effective in building their foundation of interconnectedness and shared humanity.

- Community service need not be ongoing to be effective, however, it does require contemplation and discussion to build a meaningful foundation in shared humanity.

- This practice is intended to build foundational skills needed for embracing shared humanity when suffering.

9.) PEER GROUP VS. SELF PRACTICE 3: INTERNAL POWER AND MOTIVATION VS. EXTERNAL POWER AND MOTIVATION

Learn

As teens, you have an important job—separate and leave the family! It's a time of infinite possibility when you can pursue any number of passions, interests, or identities. Applying self-compassion during this launching time involves being kind to yourself when it's rocky. Remember that you are not alone; many people before you, along with you, and long after you will also go through this passage from childhood to adulthood. Another thing that may help is to see where your power and motivation come from. Extrinsic motivation and power are people, rules, standards, and expectations outside of you that influence your behavior. To offset the impact of extrinsic power and motivation, think about the ways you have power over yourself, and the motivation that truly comes from within. Attuning to both internal and external sources of power and motivation invites self-respect, and cultivates more inner power.

Practice: Internal Power and Motivation vs. External Power and Motivation

If you have **internal** power with friends, meaning you motivate yourself and drive your own behaviors in that area, put a checkmark in that column. If you also have external power and motivation imposed upon you, meaning your friends tell you what to do and compel you to do it, check the **external** column, too. You can check both columns, or neither column for each area—whatever best applies to you.

Area of your life	Internal power and motivation	External power and motivation
With parents		
With teachers		
With friends		
With siblings		
Sports		
Art		
Music		
Games		

Reflect

- Discuss this differentiation between sources of power and motivation with your teen. Have they thought about this before?

- Does your teen find any sources of internal power? Highly impacted teens (including depressed, traumatized, and stressed teens) may not be able to find any inner power. See if you can suggest some areas.

Modification

- We all have the power of choice. For those teens that don't find any examples of internal power, or have difficulty doing so, switch the discussion to one of choice.

- Ask: Where do you have the power to make a choice in your life? For example, teens have the power to decide when and if they do their homework. They can choose to cut class or attend, to persevere or quit.

- Just looking at the topic of free choice widens perspective to include internal power, even if the connection isn't made consciously or verbally, in this immediate moment.

- It becomes the foundation for future learning about internal power and motivation, regardless of whether or not teens continue to practice self-compassion.

10.) PEER GROUP VS. SELF PRACTICE 4: BEING TOUGH TO BELONG VS. CULTIVATING INNER STRENGTH WITH SELF-COMPASSION

Learn

One way people gain membership in a group is by conforming and complying. For teens, this is a very real developmental milestone to navigate. Teens move from complying with their families to conforming to their peer group as a means of belonging. Group membership offers benefits of safety and protection. When humans were more primitive, living in groups protected them from predators and offered greater likelihood of survival through shared chores. Though we don't live with this type of predation anymore, our brains haven't gotten the memo yet. Teens still want to belong to their peer group, and sometimes doing so requires them to act in ways that are inauthentic. For example, teens who are gang involved may commit crimes in order to be initiated into the group that comes to replace broken families. In this case, the act of "being tough" can lead to criminal behavior in the most extreme cases. To mitigate the negative effects of "being tough" to belong, teach your teen about inner strength. It is always there, like an infinite stream to be tapped into as needed. Inner strength is the willingness and commitment to do the right thing, especially when it is hard.

Practice

- This matrix includes some examples that differentiate between "being tough" and harnessing "inner strength."

- See if you can complete the matrix on the next page and fill it in with any domains, or areas of your life, where you've had "inner strength" or had to "be tough" to belong.

Reflect

- Does doing the right thing come easily to you? How so?

- Does "inner strength" and "being tough" ever feel the same?

BEING TOUGH VS. INNER STRENGTH

Domain	Examples of "Being Tough"	Examples of "Inner Strength"
Sports	Running a race when you have a fever	Missing the race because you have a fever
School	Staying up all night to complete homework	Acknowledging it is too hard or too much
Friends	Going to four parties in one weekend	Going to one party; studying for exams; getting enough rest
Moral issues	Staying silent	Speaking up in the face of injustice
Peer pressure	Stealing, when friends do it and tell you to as well, in order to belong	Declaring that stealing is wrong even if it causes a rift with others

(11.) LAUNCHING PRACTICE 1: INNER DRIVES – OUTER PULLS

Learn

Adolescence is a time of great change, as brains and bodies gear up for adulthood. Moving from dependence to interdependence can be a time of inner and outer conflict. Self-compassionate teens see this aspect of their experience with kindness, and benefit from exploring the different pulls exerted upon, and within, them.

Practice

In the chart below, find examples of Inner Drives (anything that comes from inside you) and Outer Pulls (motivation, demands, and requirements imposed by others) for the each of the 5 categories listed in the column to the left. Write down Inner Drives you have about launching—going from being a teen to an independent adult. Then write down any Outer Pulls you experience around launching in the column to the right. Continue this process until you've identified Inner Drives and Outer Pulls for each of the 5 categories:

1. Self-regulation—anything you do to stay calm, alert, and balanced.

2. Peer group vs. self—the things you do alone vs. the things you do with friends

3. Launching—going from being a teen to an adult

4. Creativity—anything you do that inspires creativity or is creative

5. Sensation and novelty seeking—things you enjoy or are pulled to try that involve seeking out new things, sensations, experiences, and opportunities.

If you don't have an example for everything, it's ok, just try to reflect on all the categories, and see where you have Inner Drives and Outer Pulls.

Reflect

• There are many ways our inner wants, desires, and needs conflict with outer powers, such as parents, school, and culture. Taking time to inventory the inner and outer conflicts relieves associated suffering by honoring it.

• What did you notice about these conflicts as you completed the practice?

• Some teens have more conflicts than others. It is not necessary to judge oneself by the number of conflicts that arise. Just noticing and describing them are important steps to reducing suffering with self-compassion because it increases mindful awareness.

Category (self-regulation; peer group vs. self; launching; creativity; sensation and novelty seeking)	Inner Drives	Outer Pulls
Launching	Independence: I want and am capable of more freedom.	School and parents still make my schedule for me!
Sensation and novelty seeking	I want to try new things; exciting and adventurous experiences.	My parents, school, and culture feel it is too dangerous.

12. LAUNCHING PRACTICE 2: THE UPS AND DOWNS OF GOING FROM CHILD TO ADULT

Learn

There are new adventures, freedoms, and privileges that come with the teen years. These gains can be very exciting and fun! On the other hand, there are aspects of being a teen that continue to feel unfair and frustrating. The following practice, invites you to examine both the ups and downs of this period. This self-reflective practice promotes mindful awareness with self-kindness around changes most teens go through.

Practice

In the chart below, list all the cool, positive, and fun things about being a teen in the left column, Ups of being a teen. In the next column, under Downs of being a teen, list all the things you can think of that suck about being a teenager. There are no right or wrong answers, nor a minimum or maximum you need to find, just allow it to flow, until there isn't anything left.

Ups of being a teen	Downs of being a teen

Reflect

The main objective of this self-reflective practice is for you to explore the positive and negative aspects of your teen years. There aren't any right or wrong answers.

(13.) LAUNCHING PRACTICE 3: VULNERABILITY IN CHILDHOOD VS. ADULTHOOD

Learn

Brene Brown has influenced the discourse on vulnerability by expressing it in simple terms. She wrote, "Vulnerability sounds like truth and feels like courage. Truth and courage aren't always comfortable, but they are never weakness." She also reminds us of two more things:

1. Vulnerability is the birthplace of creativity.

2. It is also the road to courage.

When it comes to teens, the essence of vulnerability changes from moment to moment, as a function of the maturational process. In childhood, vulnerability is linked to dependency. In adulthood, vulnerability is not as commonly linked to dependency (but can be, as in the case of codependency and abusive relations). In adulthood, vulnerability is related to authenticity, "showing up" with the courage to be your true self, even and especially when that true self is at risk of being hurt and/or rejected.

Parents, educators, and clinicians can help teens mature into adulthood with courage and strength in the face of vulnerability. When they are empowered to face their own vulnerabilities, it creates open tenderness with the vulnerability of others, particularly dependent children who may come into their lives in the future, when they are adults. Ultimately, cultivating strength and courage in the face of vulnerability is a self-compassion practice because it fortifies people when they suffer. Painful times are, by definition, vulnerable times. Promoting skills to bravely face vulnerability, with kind concern and tenderness, is one road to self-compassionate living. It starts with facing one's own vulnerability with self-kindness, and extends to others through the concepts of shared humanity and interconnectedness.

Practice

This is a guided meditation, intended to be followed immediately with a writing practice. Please allow ample time for both parts of this practice, as the guided meditation prepares teens to open up to areas that may be defended against. Teens aren't likely to get defensive, but rather it may be emotionally difficult for them when defenses loosen and vulnerabilities are exposed and addressed. Doing so without adequate release can be harmful.

Materials required:

Paper
Pen

Offer the following instructions:

- Close your eyes, if you feel comfortable doing so. If not, settle your gaze downward, and fix it on a single place. Try not to move your gaze even if something distracts you. Allow your vision to blur as you focus on my voice.

- Settle into your body, and begin to notice your breath.

- Take a deep breath in through your nose, feeling the air around your nostrils as it enters, and notice it fill your belly.

- Exhale through your mouth.

- Take another deep breath through your nose, and allow the air to fill your belly. This time, hold the breath until I tell you to release it. (Count to ten.)

- Exhale through your mouth.

- Repeat this deep breath into the belly, for a 10-second count, two more times.

- Focus your attention on your toes. Feel each one, and imagine a yellow or white light on each toe. You may notice the lights moving along your toes, or all lit up at once.

- Turn your attention to your ankles, relaxing them, and noticing them.

- Moving upward now, feel your calves. Notice them and tell them to relax.

- Your thighs also benefit from your attention, send some love by using your imagination to soothe them.

- Move your attention to your hips, butt, and lower back. When you visualize these parts of your body, they receive nourishment so they can continue thriving and serving you.

- Focus on your back, upper back, and shoulders, let them relax and soften. Drop your shoulders, and straighten your neck if needed.

- Bring your attention to your head, eyes, and ears, jaw, and cheeks. Let them relax too.

- Take three deep cleansing breaths—in through the nose, and out through the mouth.

- When you are ready, open your eyes.

With pen and paper already available, invite your teen to write whatever comes to mind in reference to this statement:

"Being a child and vulnerable is. . ."

Reflect

- There is a qualitative difference between being vulnerable as a child and being vulnerable as an adult.

- This practice invites teens to explore *only* the vulnerability of a child. The comparison is introduced in this practice, but the vulnerability of being an adult isn't one a teen can explore yet, as they haven't quite reached independence.

- By establishing the difference between vulnerability in childhood vs. in adulthood, the skills required for facing it are encouraged.

- Moreover, the strength of facing childhood vulnerability is promoted with this practice, and lies at the heart of authentic self-kindness.

- Self-compassion includes self-kindness in the face of pain and suffering.

- Since pain and suffering are also moments of vulnerability, they offer practice opportunities for inner strength when self-compassion is needed most.

- This practice prepares teens for deeper practices that heal wounds at different stages of childhood. Following this with the Stop and Soothe practice (Chapter 8, Practice 3) would be a profound step toward self-healing.

14. LAUNCHING PRACTICE 3: SELF-COMPASSION FOR ANGRY AND RESISTANT TEENS

Learn

Moving from childhood to adulthood is associated with increased freedom and awareness. For some teens, this can be a painful point as the restrictions they still have to face do not resonate with the adults they are becoming, leading to anger and rebellion. In more troubling cases, the contradictions adults present to children become apparent in the later teen years and cause legitimate, yet culturally invalidated, teen anger.

Resistance causes suffering. The Buddha told a story about the pain caused by being hit by an arrow. The pain of the injury is the first cause of suffering. Often people impose a second injury upon themselves by resisting the suffering of the first injury. The Buddha continued the story by calling resistance to pain the second arrow we shoot at ourselves.

Practice

- Share the Buddha's story about the two arrows with your teen.

- Invite your teen to examine the root causes of his or her pain and suffering.

- Resistance and rebellion are natural aspects of adolescent development and worthy of being honored.

- Honoring teen angst and resistance with curiosity is a preliminary step toward giving your teen permission to be present with difficult feelings.

- The second step arises when anger and resistance are allowed free expression and exploration.

- Allow for free expression of the nature and causes of teen anger and difficult feelings, without judging and/or intervening to enforce rules and compliance.

- Mantra for anger:

  "My anger is worthy, and I am okay even when enraged. Experiencing my anger in the present moment is part of being human."

- Explain that the shadow includes the parts of ourselves that some may think of as negative—such as jealousy, anger, envy, and disgust.

- They are normal and common experiences in all of us, and equally deserving of attention, just like the good parts.

- Integrating the shadow is a way of making friends with difficult feelings, which is a self-compassionate approach to anger.

- It is one way of eliminating the second arrow injury described by the Buddha.

Reflect

- Teens develop self-compassion in the face of anger when they are assisted in facing it.

- All too often anger is associated with intensity and fear resulting in avoidance.

- Avoiding anger is a form of resistance, which causes self-destructive behaviors.

(15.) LAUNCHING PRACTICE 4: THE WAYS I AM STILL A CHILD; THE WAYS I AM ALREADY AN ADULT

Learn

One teen challenge is negotiating the gap between childhood dependency and adult interdependence. It's a tricky transition to make because subtle dependencies still exist while teens emancipate. The following practice will help you become mindful about this gap, so you can offer yourself self-kindness when it gets rough.

Practice

Still a child	Already an adult
Not allowed to stay alone overnight	Can drive a car
Still need permission to go anywhere—must account for whereabouts	Can go places alone

Reflect

- Did you notice any contradictions while filling out this practice sheet?

- Acknowledging the challenges of going from childhood to adulthood is self-compassionate because it involves mindful awareness for subtle causes of growing pain. Struggles are a natural part of emerging out of childhood, and into adulthood. Natural courses of development also connect us to each other, in shared humanity.

(16.) CREATIVITY PRACTICE 1: MANDALA

Learn

Teens suffer when they don't have opportunities to express themselves creatively, and creativity has the power to heal pain and suffering. For both reasons, it is important to empower teens to find the medium that best suits them.

Some teens enjoy:

- Digital art

- Doodles

- Making videos

- Coloring pages (adult coloring books, such as: *Sit the F*ck Down and Color* or *Calm the F*ck Down*)

- Drawing

- Music—listening, singing, writing, playing an instrument

- Writing

Material needed:

- Bristol board

- Magazines

- Markers or colored pencils

- Scissors

- Glue

Practice

- In the center of the Bristol board, draw a circle.

- Fill the circle with pictures, words, and drawings that speak to your creativity.

- Let the images and phrases that fill the circle be a representation of all creative things, media, and activities that inspire you.

- It's okay if you don't fill the mandala today. You can come back to it at any time, if you find something you like.

- Use this activity to discover the creative outlets that contribute to your well-being.

- There is no right or wrong activity to include.

Reflect

- Encouraging all forms and practices of creativity heals wounds, inspires passion, innovation, and courage in the face of vulnerability.

- Practices that promote creative exploration are self-compassionate because they heal, while leading to thriving in adolescence and adulthood, and provide joy, as well as meaningful existence.

Coloring Page

Self-Compassion Training
for Teens with School Challenges

School challenges in the teen years include stress, performance demands, academic failure, college competition, not performing according to one's potential, procrastination, and bullying. These issues can be addressed in a holistic manner with self-compassion at the center.

The activities in this chapter are suitable for all populations and concerns.

1. MULTIPLE INTELLIGENCES

Learn

Students benefit from learning about the multiple intelligences (Gardner, 1993) as a means of turning mindfully toward their strengths and weaknesses. Doing so is an act of self-compassion as it leads to greater clarity about oneself, as well as opportunities for shared humanity and self-kindness.

Gardner proposed eight different types of intelligence, much more than is measured on IQ and/or academic achievement tests. They are:

1. **Musical Intelligence** = music smart

2. **Kinesthetic Intelligence** = body smart

3. **Linguistic Intelligence** = word smart

4. **Interpersonal Intelligence** = people smart

5. **Intrapersonal Intelligence** = self smart

6. **Visual-Spatial Intelligence** = picture smart

7. **Logical Intelligence** = logic smart

8. **Naturalist Intelligence** = nature smart

Practice

- Invite teens to draw eight bars of any height representing their self-perception on each of the eight intelligences.

- The bars need not correspond exactly to your teen's actual intelligence level, but rather reflect the teen's view of him- or herself on each kind of intelligence, relative to the other kinds of intelligence.

- The key here is for teens to log their *relative* strengths and weaknesses related to the multiple intelligences.

- Explain to teens that assessing their abilities and interests from their perspective is not only an act of self-empathy, but also self-compassion as it can mitigate suffering in school.

Reflect

- Self-assessing strengths and weaknesses with loving kindness and awareness of shared humanity can reduce self-criticism, shaming, and humiliation.

- Current methods of assessment do not value self-empathy and self-reflection, and as a result teens suffer with the judgments others impose on their academic efforts.

MULTIPLE INTELLIGENCES GRAPH

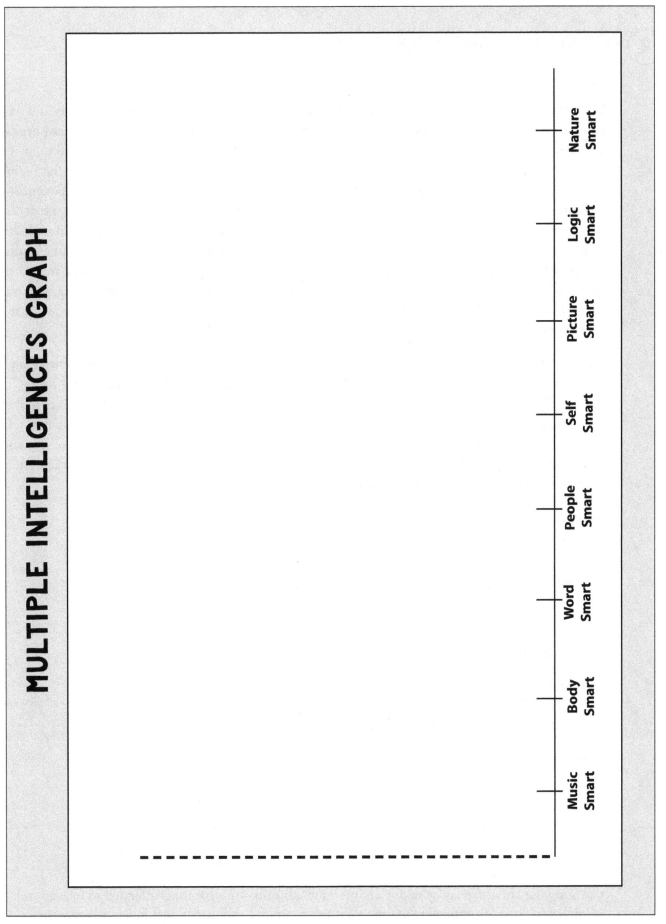

Music Smart | Body Smart | Word Smart | People Smart | Self Smart | Picture Smart | Logic Smart | Nature Smart

2. CREATIVITY AND SELF-COMPASSION

Learn

Experts agree (Siegel, 2013; Robinson & Aronica, 2015; Lichtman, 2014) that creativity is a key component of growing young minds. From a self-compassion perspective, being creative is the purpose and meaning of human life; it is a universal human need and capacity that heals and soothes, while promoting problem-solving skills. According to Kaufman (2013), creativity arises when the brain's default network is activated. This type of mind-wandering activity is a shared human experience—all minds wander—and is associated with solving problems using new strategies and approaches. Recognizing this in the teen years may decrease the pathologization of a wandering mind and also inspire healthy ways of managing it. Cultivating space, time, and practices for creativity is an essential component of healthy living, and also of training teens in self-compassion. It gives teens a way to let their minds wander with purpose. As schools replace art, drama, music, and woodworking with test preparation activities, the responsibility of cultivating creativity falls on teens themselves, with the support of adults like you!

When teens spend time creating, they also activate the natural state of flow. Mihaly Csikszentmihalyi, author of *Flow: The Psychology of Optimal Experience*, introduced us to the science behind being "in the zone." It is the state of being absorbed in an activity, and experiencing joy. Siegel (2013) describes it as being immersed in an activity to such a point that time is lost, self-consciousness abates, and the distinction between self and activity dissolves. This is a state of self-compassion because it is also when the highest level of self-kindness can arise. Teaching teens about this state, and how to achieve it, decreases suffering, and is therefore an act of self-compassion.

Practice

Read this to your teen:

- Begin by settling into your body, and taking in a beautiful deep breath.

- Allow it to fill your belly, and then hold it for a count of three.

- And exhale…

- Repeat this beautiful breathing for two more breaths.

- Tune in to your head and tell all the muscles to relax.

- Tell your forehead, eyes, ears, mouth, and chin to relax.

- Notice your neck and shoulders, tell them to relax and loosen.

- Invite your shoulders to drop and settle comfortably into this moment.

- Feel your arms lengthen and loosen as you tell them it's also okay to let go.

- Allow your chest to relax by taking an intentional breath—this breath is intended to release your lungs and chest for optimal relaxation. With this mindful and intentional inhale, observe the sensations in your chest as it relaxes and infuses you with creativity, releases any blocks, and moves air flow through you.

- Focus on your upper back, tell it to relax by softly saying, "Relax upper back."

- Move your attention downward to your middle and lower back, tell them to relax, too.

- Focus on your belly, and tell it to relax. See a little box in there. Notice the outside of the box, the colors and design, and trust we will come back to it soon.

- Relax your groin, hips, buttocks, and thighs by telling them it's okay to relax.

- Place your attention on your knees, and tell them to relax.

- Tell your shins and calves to relax.

- Tell your ankles and feet to relax too.

- Feel your feet heavy and anchored into the floor.

- Return your attention to the little box in your belly.

- This is a special box that we all possess, like a heart that specializes in creativity and flow rather than pumping blood throughout the body.

- When you're ready, use your attention and intention to open the box. You can open it in your mind's eye, or use a silent command, like:

"Open up special box of flow and creativity."

- *Pause*

- This special box of creativity and flow is the seat of your talents and gifts. Now that it is open, your talents and gifts will develop even further, and make themselves known to you if you don't already feel connected to them.

Reflect

- What does your special box look like?

- Did you notice anything when yours opened up?

- Have you ever felt like you were in the flow, or in the zone, where time flew by and you seemed able to concentrate and focus for long periods of time?

- Being in flow, or in the groove or zone, is the space where creativity is alive. Making time to go there, and valuing it, are self-compassion practices because they feed the human need to create.

- Flow heals, in addition to being one pathway to innovation, both of which contribute kindly to being and sharing in the human experience.

- Reassure teens that it is natural for talents, gifts, and passionate interests to arise in different ways and times. There is no set expectation for when and how they will come to learn about their gifts.

- Being attuned to, and inviting, talents and gifts to present themselves is how we begin cultivating them. Trust the process has already begun even if you do not see results yet.

3. DIFFERENT KINDS OF CREATIVITY

Learn

There are many different ways of demonstrating creativity. The new connections that arise when we learn are examples of learning that we refer to as "mini-c." Another kind of creativity occurs when we solve everyday problems, which is called "little-c." The creativity associated with professional endeavors is called "Pro-c," while creativity springing forth from those with eminent talent is "Big-C." (Kaufman, 2013.)

Practice

- For each box in this figure, fill in examples of your creativity. For example:

  a. mini-c creativity refers to things like solving math equations, teasing out similarities and differences in history facts.

  b. little-c creativity refers to figuring out a life problem without guidance, or prior instruction, and using common sense to find new ways of doing things in daily life.

  c. Pro-c creativity is the kind that occurs when a scientist makes a new discovery, or lawyer creates a brief.

  d. Big-C is related to prodigious talent or eminence.

  e. It may be hard to find examples for Pro-c and Big-C kinds of creativity, that's okay! The important thing is now you know more about the different kinds of creativity so you can identify yours when it appears.

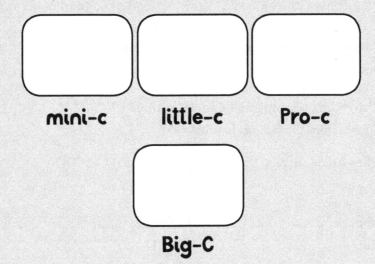

Reflect

- Do you think of yourself as a creative person? Why or why not?

- Some people think they just aren't creative, and/or don't have talent. This is a myth, and that when held as truth is actually unkind to oneself and all of humanity too. When you remember your inherent and prolific creativity, you are practicing self-kindness with tenderness for all of humanity too.

4. CREATIVITY, COMMUNICATION, AND COMPASSION

Learn

How we handle conflicts and challenges also invites creativity. When we build each other up, we heal and offer self-compassion by spreading kindness through the interconnectedness of all people. We have the potential to be creative in language by using words that warm the heart. Marshall Rosenberg, the creator of *Non-Violent Communication (NVC),* also known as compassionate communication, promoted communication and conflict resolution with empathy and compassion for ourselves, and others, in dialogues. This method of speaking and listening relies on a template for identifying needs, and seeking to meet them in a pro-social way. NVC's premise is that it is universally human to have needs, and that people suffer or hurt others when their needs are not met. Teens who learn NVC practice self-compassion and creativity in communication by verbalizing needs, and by resolving differences in kind, compassionate, respectful, and empathic ways.

Practice

Self-Compassionate speech consists of four parts:

1. What is happening right now? What do you notice in this moment?

2. What are you feeling?

3. What is your universal human need?

4. What request can you make, either of yourself or another person?

Step 1: **What do you see happening in yourself or others?**
State it.

Step 2: **What feeling accompanies your observation?**
(Choose from the feelings lists below.)

Feelings when needs are met:

Alert	Energized	Joyous
Comfortable	Fulfilled	Positive
Confident	Grateful	Proud
Curious	Happy	Trusting
Eager	Hopeful	

Feelings when needs are unmet:

Afraid	Discomfort	Irritation
Annoyed	Discouraged	Loneliness
Angry	Distress	Nervousness
Anxiety	Frustration	Overwhelm
Confused	Helplessness	Reluctance
Depressed	Hopelessness	Sadness
Disappointed	Impatience	Worry

Step 3: What need is not being met in your observation?
(Choose a need from the lists of basic human needs that follow.)

Some basic human needs:

Physical needs

- Air
- Food and water
- Movement
- Protection
- Rest
- Recreation
- Shelter
- Touch and affection

Freedom

- Choosing and pursuing dreams, goals, values

Integrity

- Authenticity
- Creativity
- Meaning
- Self-worth

Need for joy and celebration:

- To celebrate the creation of life and dreams fulfilled
- Play
- Fun
- Laughter

Interdependence

- Acceptance
- Intimacy
- Community
- Kindness and respect

- Empathy
- Love
- Trust

- Understanding
- Warmth
- Assistance

Spiritual communion

- Beauty
- Inspiration
- Peace and harmony

Step 4: **What is your request, in order to meet your need? Is it made of yourself, or of another person?**

Using the template that follows, observe the feeling and unmet need, then state a request. Use the four steps you read about previously to fill in the four blanks below:

When I see/hear (state the observation) _____.

I feel (state emotion) _____,
because I need (state the need) _____.

My request of (other/self) is _____.

(This request shall be directly linked to the unmet need.)

Reflect

- The words we use have the power to bring us together and create conflict. What is it like to have a template for speaking up about your needs, wants, feelings, and requests?

- It takes a lot of practice, attention to yourself, your needs and feelings, to be a self-compassionate communicator. Would you be willing to invest time in this way of speaking? Do you have any buddies (of any age) who may wish to learn along with you?

5. CHOOSING SELF-COMPASSIONATE WORDS

Learn

Some words harm, others heal. Taking the time to choose words that bring kindness, respect, empathy, and compassion for oneself and others is an act of self-compassion. When our words bring us together with others, they become elements of kindness as bonds among people. With healing properties, words have the potential to reduce suffering when chosen carefully.

Practice

Think about these words:

- Provoked
- Unappreciated
- Unheard
- Unseen

- Attacked
- Manipulated
- Misunderstood
- Abused

These words speak to what we *think* another person is doing to us to cause suffering. It can seem intentional and deliberate on their part, but unless we go inside their minds, we can't know for sure.

Now, reflect on a circumstance in your life where you are in conflict with another person. Do any of the words in the previous list apply to your conflict? If so, please describe the conflict. Please elaborate the ways in which there is division and separation between you and the other person.

_____

_____

_____

_____

_____

In compassionate communication, we focus on needs and feelings because they are happen to most everyone. Division and conflict are common, yet unhealthy and unnatural states of being. The language used reflects the intention and approach to an issue, and also impacts the outcome. Self-compassionate language can be used when conflict arises with others. Instead of focusing on division, conflict, and harm, self-compassionate language promotes connection, the expression of feelings, and need meeting.

Now, reflect again on the same circumstance in your life where you are in conflict with another person. Instead of focusing on the division, harm, and opposition between you and the other person, think of your unmet needs and how it makes you feel. For example, if you feel manipulated when your friend doesn't agree to make plans until the last minute, you can focus on the harm and distance caused by calling your friend's actions "manipulative." A self-compassionate approach to the same situation might look like this:

You need advance planning to feel good and happy about making plans with your friend. In this reframe, no one is manipulating anyone, instead needs, feelings, and connection become the focus. Most friends want to stay friends. Framing problems in terms of your needs, rather than how they harmed you creates lasting bonds. On the lines below, write about a time you were having conflict with a friend. This time, use words that reflect your feelings about the needs you had that were not being met. Discuss it in ways that keep you and the other person together, rather than separate and in conflict.

_____

_____

_____

_____

_____

Reflect

- It takes courage to look at unmet needs and corresponding feelings because it elicits vulnerability.
- Ask a trusted person to help you see what needs you have that may not be met.
- We become stronger when we focus on needs and feelings; our relationships become tighter too.
- Many people take a minimum of six months of active practice to become proficient with compassionate communication. Give yourself all the time you need, and forgive yourself when your language is not self-compassionate or compassionate.

(6.) EMPATHIC LISTENING

Learn

How we interpret the things we hear impacts feelings, beliefs, and thoughts. Judgment about the information we receive is the cause of great suffering. One way to mitigate personal suffering is through empathic listening. It follows the same template as compassionate communication, and is used for clarifying and confirming your impression of another person's speech. Confirming your understanding of what someone else is saying is an act of self-compassion because it gives you a chance to work through misunderstandings right away. Minimizing misunderstandings with others is a source of self-compassion because it reduces suffering.

Practice

- When listening to your friends, siblings, teachers, and parents, use the template that follows to see if you are truly getting the gist of what they are saying.

- We think we get what others say, but often it is a false assumption filtered through our lens of perception and experience.

- Refer to the Selective Attention activity in Chapter 1, to see just how much is missed, even when people think they are paying close attention.

Use this template to practice.

I saw/heard you (state the observed behavior/action) _____ .

Do you feel (state observed emotion) _____ , because you need (state possible need) _____ ?

Would you like (state request on behalf of other) _____ ?

Reflect

- How is it to listen deeply and rephrase your partner's words using a template?

- Does it feel cumbersome to repeat the other person's words? Does it take a lot of time? Does it feel stupid and robotic?

- How about conflict and misunderstanding, do they take time to sort out?

- Confirming the essence of what you heard in what others' mean to say can eliminate a lot of suffering and meet needs, while deepening bonds and closeness.

(7.) SELF-COMPASSIONATE STUDENT VISION BOARD

Learn

A vision board is a collage and collection of words or drawings that represent a vision held for one's future. By invoking the imagination along with the visual processing aspects of cutting, pasting, and arranging, teens can wire their brains to favorably influence their outcomes. Vision boards represent an opportunity for creativity as well as reflection on what teens truly desire and want for themselves. This vision board activity prompts teens to consider the kind of student they would be if self-compassion was part of their mind-set and way of being/relating.

Practice

Materials:

- Magazines
- Bristol board
- Scissors
- Glue
- Markers

Read these instructions to your teen:

- Take a few deep breaths and become present in this moment.

- Allow images, thoughts, ideas, fantasies, wishes, dreams, and more to float into awareness.

- Consider the following statement:

What would I be like if I were a self-compassionate student?

- Create a vision board by selecting images/statements/words from the magazines provided.

- Allow yourself to be guided and pulled by whatever fancies you.

- There is no rhyme of reason to how you place the images, just follow your heart.

- When you finish, step back and take a good long look at your creation.

- See if a story or theme emerges that makes sense to you.

Reflect

- The innermost wisest part of every person already knows why they are here.

- Meeting potential and becoming aligned with one's unique calling relies on surrendering to the part within that already knows.

- This vision board is an exercise in cultivating the innermost wisest part of your teen. It helps teens practice surrendering to not knowing how they know, and yet letting themselves flow with it anyway.

8. WHAT THREE EXCUSES KEEP YOU FROM BEING CREATIVE, BEING HONEST, AND HAVING THE LIFE YOU WANT?

Learn

Often, people are their own worst enemy. Self-criticism is employed as a strategy to promote improved performance, however, it is not a very effective way of reaching potential. By facing excuses, self-criticism is extinguished. There is little oxygen to fuel it when courage and bravery reign over excuses. This practice is a one-off activity you can use to begin confronting the excuses you make that keep you from reaching your potential.

Practice

List three excuses that keep you from being creative:

1. _____

2. _____

3. _____

List three excuses that keep you from being honest:

1. _____

2. _____

3. _____

List three excuses that keep you from having the life you truly want:

1. _____

2. _____

3. _____

Reflect

• For teens, there is a tricky balance between your dependence and the growing independence.

• This practice introduces you to the excuses that hamper your inner locus of control.

• If any conflicts emerge between the life you want to live, your creativity, and honesty and the values, beliefs, and customs of your parents and culture, suffering is likely. To mitigate this suffering with self-compassion, you need a safe place to explore autonomy needs vs community needs, and the level of dependence and independence needed in your life.

WHAT KIND OF STUDENT/PERSON DO I WANT TO BE?

Learn

In the previous practice, teens explored the excuses, or barriers, to their creativity, honesty, and living the life they want most. This practice invites teens to explore the role they lead as students or people in the world. Taking the time to reflect on this helps teens become mindful and bring self-kindness to their dreams and aspirations.

Practice

Reflect on the person/student you want to be. Describe in detail, in the space provided below:

_____

_____

_____

_____

_____

_____

Reflect

- Are there any stereotypes that impact the person you are and wish to be?

- Does the culture support you being whom you wish to be?

- Are there ways you need to say no to things/people/experiences in order to be true to yourself?

10. <u>**WHAT DO I LIKE TO DO?**</u>

Learn

When teens only do the things their parents, teachers, and culture tell them is right for them, it can cause suffering. Reflecting and evaluating on the activities you enjoy creates a treasure trove of ways to mediate difficult times. Moreover, the time spent on activities that bring enjoyment are also likely to lead to moments of flow,[2] or being in the zone of optimal performance. *"Time you enjoy wasting, was not wasted"* (Troly-Curtin, 1912) is a powerful quote, reminding us that the road to greatness is both long and winding, and may not always seem like it is going anywhere at all.

4 Tips:

1. Set goals for yourself.
2. Be absorbed in the activities you are involved in.
3. Pay attention to what's going on; avoid distractions of self-awareness and self-criticism or self-judgment.
4. Learn to enjoy the immediate experience.

The following self-reflective practice promotes mindfully becoming aware of one's interests, qualities, and abilities with kindness. Seeking out learning opportunities that are personally meaningful is correlated with flow, passion, and happiness. For these reasons, it is very important to help teens take the time to learn about themselves and their true interests as it mitigates suffering.

Practice

- What are all your good qualities? We're talking about your gifts, talents, superpowers, and righteous skills. Don't hold back, just brag away.

Write them all here:

_____   _____

_____   _____

_____   _____

_____   _____

_____   _____

_____   _____

_____   _____

Now, circle (or highlight) the top three qualities you love most about yourself.

Are there any situations, clubs, classes, camps, schools, programs, or places you could join that would promote or grow your three top superpowers?
List them here:

_____   _____

_____   _____

_____   _____

_____   _____

_____   _____

_____   _____

- For this practice, there are no wrong answers. Widen your imagination so more possibilities can become available to you. You don't have to do all the things that come to mind; creating a longer list offers more chances of finding the best fit for your unique gifts and talents.

Reflect

- What was it like to think of your good qualities?
- The more time spent focusing on the good within, the more it grows. Could you see yourself focusing on at least three to five good things about yourself every day? (Focusing means reminding yourself of your gifts and/or spending time on them.)

11. WHAT MAKES ME FEEL BETTER WHEN I FAIL?

Learn

The stress of school (assignments, tests, college applications, and more) leads teens to experience failure at some point. Coping with failure involves tapping into activities that self-soothe. Self-compassion involves mindfully acknowledging failure, responding to it with self-acceptance and kindness, and remembering that it is a universal experience we all face at some point. The following activity is intended to help you discover the activities, thoughts, actions, and practices you can use to feel better when facing failure.

Practice

When failure occurs, some people learn and move forward trusting that the experience was fruitful for the learning that occurred. In other cases, people can feel really badly. When you feel badly, what makes you feel better? List everything here:

_____

_____

_____

_____

_____

_____

Reflect

- Take time to practice any or all of these when failure arises, or even when times are good. These same practices also increase well-being.

- Being able to let go of negative thoughts, feelings, and beliefs is an act of self-kindness. It reduces suffering, and is therefore also self-compassionate. By focusing attention on the ways you can feel good and happy, it leaves less room for the negative stuff.

(12.) CELEBRATING FAILURE

Learn

FAIL is an acronym that stands for First Attempt In Learning. One approach to failure that embraces learning, growth, and forward movement is to celebrate it. There are many good reasons to celebrate failure, chief among them is that you learn what doesn't work when failure occurs. Creating customs, rituals, and celebrations to encourage more failure helps teens gain confidence with failing, which increases resiliency.

Practice

• Celebrate failures.

• Create festive sounds, hand movements, slogans, and cheers to use when your teen fails.

• Involve family members, classmates, and others when and wherever possible in celebrating failure.

• Treat failure as worthy as success.

Reflect

• What is it like for you and your teen to reconceptualize failure in this way?

• Discuss the times failure led to something else, something unexpected, perhaps even better.

• Sometimes failure is a signal to slow down. Has your teen ever experienced failure, and found that slowing down helps?

(13.) WHAT DON'T I LIKE?

Learn

It is just as important to know what doesn't work for you, as it is to know what does. There is a biological basis to avoiding things we don't like. With regard to things we ingest, those that taste bitter may be poisonous. It is an evolutionary feature of toxic foods, plants, and chemicals by interfering with consumption. How do we know if an experience, activity, or adventure is good for us? We can't taste it to find out, and sometimes the things that are good for some people are really bad for others. For example, peanuts are a good source of protein, especially for vegans and vegetarians. On the other hand, peanuts are lethal to those with nut allergies. In the following activity, teens take time to list things they dislike. This inventory serves as a pathway to discovering "allergies" to certain activities or events. For other sensory related activities, see Chapter 3 and Chapter 11.

Practice

• What are all the things you dislike and avoid? Don't resist, just complain away. Feel free to include things you must do. Write them all here:

_____

_____

_____

_____

_____

_____

_____

• Circle (or highlight) the top three things you avoid no matter what.

In the lines provided, explain in detail why you avoid and dislike these three things.

1. _____

_____

_____

2. _____

_____

_____

3. _____

_____

_____

Reflect

- There is nothing to be ashamed of for disliking and avoiding certain things.

- Please remain judgment free about these nonpreferred things. Just like people with nut allergies can't have peanuts for good reason, there is probably a very good reason why your teen avoids the things they dislike. Discovering those reasons can be freeing because then teens don't have to try to be good at something they don't like or want to be good at.

- This ability to discriminate between preferred and nonpreferred activities is critical for long-term career success and happiness.

14. DECLARING YES AND NO

Learn

Now that your teen has discovered their likes and dislikes, empowerment arises from being able to say "yes" and embrace the good, while saying "no" to things that cause suffering. Limit setting, boundaries, and the ability to say "no" are critical components of self-compassion, as well as compassion for others. All teens need the right to say no, and preserve certain human inalienable rights. These include the rights to defend one's life, pursue healthy and loving relationships, determine what is toxic to them, and reject it in favor of a good life. The act of saying no creates room for that which is special to each individual to emerge organically. And when it does, other rights also flourish like the right to choose which stories and "truths" one believes. They also include the right to be honest with oneself, take all the time needed, live in the present moment, have silence, be silent, and surrender. The foregoing 11 declarations are influenced by Altucher and Altucher's "No Bill of Rights" (2014,) yet extend to embracing the "yeses" in life, as well as the "nos."

Declaration:	Say "YES" to...	Say "NO" to...
#1	Defending your life	Anything that is toxic to you specifically
#2	Warm, respectful, and kind relationships	People who are mean, manipulative, and rude
#3	Enjoy your talents and gifts, and any goodness that comes along	Anything that is an obstacle to your talents and gifts
#4	Respectfully prioritizing whatever you want and that which is special to you	Priorities that are not aligned with your heart's desire
#5	Creating authentic stories about the life you lead	To stories that do not reflect your authentic self
#6	To taking all the time you need, even if it is not in synch with others	To anything or anyone that rushes you
#7	Finding your truth, and taking all the time it requires	Rejecting stereotypes that aren't aligned with your truth
#8	Abundance & gratitude	The scarcity complex and living in fear
#9	Living in the present moment	Living in the past; living in the future
#10	Quiet time	Anything that is noisy or feels like a noisy distraction
#11	Surrender	The illusion that you are in control, and know what's truly happening

In the first part of this practice, adult caregivers are invited to give teens permission to say no. The freedom and power that arise from being able to decline something promotes healing, and is an act of self-kindness and self-compassion. The way teens spend their lives is largely determined by other people. If they are given three "free passes" to say no every week, for example, the impact on their functioning and future is tremendous. In the second part of the practice, teens look at the process of saying no, in order to minimize obstacles to healthy boundary and limit setting.

Practice

Part I: Permission to Say No

- Parents: consider giving teens the right to refuse three times per week.

- Teachers and clinicians: invite parents to offer their teens the right to say no.

- It's okay to set limits and exclude some things, like school and homework.

- One way for teens to say no, and still respect responsibilities and household obligations is by saying, "Not right now," and then indicating when a task will be completed.

- Offering teens this level of empowerment demonstrates trust in their judgment, while giving them experience in setting boundaries and declining unsavory situations.

- When teens are allowed to decline requests, tasks, or temporarily defer chores, they learn how to modulate a rapidly changing world, which has essentially caused a lot of suffering.

Part II: Reflection on Saying No

(Discuss these questions with your teen, or have your teen complete this part as an inventory.)

1. What was it like to hold the power of no?

2. Have you been able to tell people in your life that something didn't quite work for you?

3. Have you found yourself forced to comply and conform in order to succeed?

4. Do you feel uncomfortable saying no?

5. Did you use any of your free passes to say no to adults in your life? If so, what was it like? Would you do it again? Why or why not?

6. Complete the following sentence fragments:

Saying no is easy because _____.

Saying no is hard because _____.

Saying yes is easy because _____.

Saying yes is hard because _____.

When I say no, I feel _____.

When I say yes, I feel _____.

When I say no, I believe the following about myself; I am _____.

When I say yes, I believe the following about myself; I am _____.

Reflect

- As adults, consider how unusual it is to turn power over to minors.

- Why do adults do so much for teens?

- Does it truly benefit them? Did you notice yourself examining your relationship with the word *no* and limit and boundary setting as you thought about it in relation to your teen?

- Have a discussion with your teen about Part II of this practice. The questions are powerful discussion starters on topics teens really need help navigating, and for which little guidance is available.

⑮ INTENTION SETTING

Learn

Here's the secret to setting and meeting goals: Intentions.

Intentions are the mental precedent to goal setting. When setting a goal, you use logic, estimation, measurement, and reasoning to figure out the steps needed to get to the end point. When making a plan to reach a goal, and life's obstacles arise, it can cause pain, suffering, anxiety, worry, frustration, despair, worthlessness, helplessness, powerlessness, and depression. Setting intentions before setting goals initiates the same process from a different angle. It invites you to speak from your heart, to the universe, without needing to have all the steps of the plan figured out yet. It is like making a wish, and surrendering to the process, then being willing to take action to set the plan later, as the details emerge. This, my friends, is the secret sauce to success.

Practice

Have your teen complete the worksheet on the next page.

Reflect

- Discuss with your teen what it is they really want in life. Is it intrinsically or extrinsically motivated?

- See if your teen can connect intention setting to school, career, health, and social emotional goals.

- If there are any challenges in your teen's life, see if they are open to setting intentions as a way of taking a small, yet highly impactful, step toward big goals.

- Turning attention to what you want, in a positive way, sets neurons firing while attentional cues are activated in accordance with the established intention. The process of setting intentions then, is literally one of igniting neurons to begin firing in patterns related to successful and desirable outcomes.

Modification

- For angry teens, or when special safety conditions can be assured for you and your teen, instead of tearing up the paper with intentions and throwing it in the trash, light it on fire.

- If safety considerations allow, let your teen handle the fire, and clean the remains after the paper stops burning.

- The act of burning intentions, and giving teens the power of fire to destroy, is laden with symbolic significance that imparts meaning at the cellular and intuitive level.

- Fire has immense power, as do intentions. When we use fire with good intentions, it creates things we need. When fire is used with negative, or no intentions, the consequences can be dire. Setting intentions is one way of establishing goals that have potential to succeed, without being derailed by unintended side effects.

DIFFERENCES BETWEEN SETTING INTENTIONS AND SETTING GOALS

	Intentions	Goals
Realistic	Maybe (less likely)	Maybe (more likely)
Logical	No	Yes
Origin	Heart centered	Judgment based
Point of motivation	Intrinsic	Extrinsic
Surrendered	Yes	No
Plan	No	Yes
Outcome oriented	Maybe	Yes
Action taken/required	No	Yes

- Think of something you want to happen. Describe it in positive terms. (i.e., "I set the intention to prepare for, and take, my next test with ease and success.)

- Intentions focus on the positive, rather than on the negative. (Avoid: "I set the intention to end world hunger." The positive flipside to that might be: "I set the intention to connect hungry people with food.")

- When setting intentions, think not only of the outcome but also about how you want to feel while doing something, or working your way through your plan toward your goal.

- Write your intention on a piece of paper using this formula (write as many intentions as you like):

"I set the following intentions freely of my own open and loving heart, for the greater good of all.

"I set the intention to _____

_____."

"I set the intention to _____

_____."

"I set the intention to _____

_____."

These are my declared intentions for today, _____ (write the date), set with my own free will."

- When you write each intention, think only about how it will come to be. Just write what your heart longs for.

- As a gentle reminder, your heart longs for big and super exciting things, so don't hold back because it seems like your wishes might be too large and/or far away.

- Intentions tend to be effective when they are spoken from our own hearts, and not through the hearts of others. Set intentions based on your own longings and desire, rather than what your parents and teachers want for you.

- One way to tell the difference between the two is that your longings are exciting and energizing; those that come from other people tend to cause anxiety, and involve the word *should*, somewhere in the mix.

- Fold up your piece of paper with the intention(s) on it, and tear it up, and throw it away in the trash.

- When you tear up the paper, let go of the wish/intention with trust that the universe will support you in achieving it.

- When we set intentions with clarity, and with the greater good in mind, you can reach your goals with ease and success.

- Setting intentions is also like taking out an insurance policy on your aspirations, hopes, and dreams. It has protective factors because it directs choice, actions, focus, and learning at a deeply subconscious level with positive vibrations.

- Unlike goal setting, intention setting involves letting go, not moving to plan, but allowing the plan to come forward.

- Setting the intention is the first step, in a series of steps, to success, and it involves a lot of patience and persistence.

- Keep setting intentions, taking action, being patient, and repeating the process over and over again.

16. "MY WORD IS MY WAND": AFFIRMING THE GOOD TO CREATE MORE GOOD AND USING POSITIVE LANGUAGE TO PROMOTE MORE GOOD

Learn

The way we speak has powerful effects to connect people in service of meeting each other's needs, and/or to destroy. The following activity is essentially a gentle reminder that the words we use generate reality. Selecting words that promote kindness and respect, while focusing on the positive is a self-compassionate practice. It mitigates suffering by co-creating a reality that is filled with joy.

Practice

- As a daily practice, write down everything you affirm in your life:

"I affirm with love and gratitude that I am _____ ."

(Fill in the blank. Here are some options: healthy, happy, safe, peaceful, empowered, prosperous, energized, calm, becoming a person I love.)

- Affirm as many things as you can every day.

- Here's the thing: you don't have to be any of the things you affirm in order to affirm them. For example, you don't need to be happy already to affirm happiness, even though that is when it is easiest. By affirming what you want, you select words that can be used to set intentions.

- If you are sick, it can be very difficult to affirm health. In that case, you can affirm that you are healing, or recovering, or mending, etc

- The key is to select states of being that you wish to have in your life.

Reflect

- Affirmations are a way of initiating a kind dialogue with yourself. They have a way of bringing light to intentions, and clarity to goals.

- Affirmations tend to be general, yet positive.

- Using kind words to speak about the foundation of your life reduces suffering by co-creating a world of abundance and success.

17. IMAGINE YOUR VERY BEST LIFE

Learn

After taking your teen through intention setting, affirmations, NVC, deeply focused self-reflection, and creativity practices, it is a great time to bring it all together! First we imagine; then we create. The act of inventing, dreaming, and fantasizing about something is a function of the imaginal sphere. That's the upside. Paul Gilbert, author of *The Compassionate Mind* (2009), explained further that the creative power of our imagination is huge. He reports on the physiological effects of being hungry and seeing a meal. Our mouths start to water upon sight of the food, gastric juices are secreted, and stomachs grumble. However, when we are hungry and no meal is available, only imagining the same meal will result in the very same physiological processes unfolding. Gilbert asks his reader to pause and consider the implications of this. Let's do that now, as well!

Imagining something causes the same biological processes to occur as living the same experience.

The downside of having powerful imagination occurs when it gets trapped in a repetitive cycle of angry, sad, worried, afraid, or anxious ideas. Rumination ensues. When teens perpetuate self-critical thinking, they activate the *limbic system*, which is also responsible for threat detection and protection. The power of imagination stuck on negative thoughts causes depression, anxiety, panic, distractibility, and overall low levels of functioning.

Alas, there is hope! Charlotte Reznick, author of *The Power of Your Child's Imagination*, guides parents, educators, and clinicians in how to use imagination to shift out of the negative realm, and into the positive. The effects of making this shift promote creativity, healing, and even realizing dreams. Reznick offers nine core tools teens can use to cultivate self-compassion. She appreciates the value and potential of, what the Buddha called the "Beginner's Mind," and offers up her tools as "magic beans," that germinate when used by teens. With regard to shifting from the negative to the positive areas of imagination, Reznick's "Healing Touch," "Healing Gaze," and especially "Healing Thought" are powerful ways for teens to instantly engage their inner storehouse of self-compassion.

Practice I

Here are a couple practices you can use with teens.

• When things go wrong, do you have a way of thinking about them over and over again? Most people do. It's called rumination, and sometimes it serves a good purpose, like when we are trying to solve a puzzle or problem. It isn't such a good thing when it perpetuates confusion, sadness, and problems in our lives. Here's how to stop the cycle of negative rumination:

1. Stop! (I know easier said than done. Now, STOP! Stop yourself.)

2. Restate the same thought, belief, or memory with a positive twist.

3. Repeat the new and positive belief, seeking memories as evidence of its truth.

4. Find activities, adventures, and learning and growth opportunities that lead the positive belief to become reality.

It's okay if you don't believe the positive reframe. It's important to just stop the rumination cycle.

Practice II

- Imagine and visualize as many details as possible about the kind of life you want right now, in one year, and in five years. Take your time to allow the images to evolve.

  Modification: Write down all the details about your one-year, five-year, and present moment life dreams.

- Repeat often to train your brain in the neural pathways needed to create the dream you want to live as your life.

Reflect

- Encourage teens to take time to imagine.

- Explore how using imagination to self-heal is possible.

- Practice Reznick's nine tools with teens as a means of giving them the "magic beans" for living their very best life, and help them grow the beans. The tools are very powerful ways of rewiring the brain so teens can shift quickly from negative to positive thinking. Find all nine tools, and more in her book, *The Power of Your Child's Imagination.*

- Invite teens to talk about their imagination.
  - Do they still access it? If so, how and when?
  - Explore reverie and daydreaming.
  - Where the mind wanders, the heart wants to be.

(18.) STOP, BE, SETTLE, AND QUIET

Learn

Recharge and restore in order to have energy for learning and creating by stopping activities, being, settling, and quieting. These four simple steps are essential self-compassion practices for teens with fast-paced lives. Teens are exposed to alarming rates of stress and pressure in high school, as well as in applying, qualifying for, and completing college. Without intentional breaks, burnout occurs—even in the teen years.

Practice

1. *Stop* all activities: Put your devices away if you can, otherwise use it to help you stop. The device can be a timer you use to set aside time for your intentional break, or it can be a source of soothing music, calming guided meditation, or something that brings you pleasure, but doesn't require effort.

2. *Be* in the moment with the full experience of stopping. Notice where your mind goes, how you feel, and if any sensations arise in your body.

3. *Settle* into your break. Enjoy the time you have intentionally set aside for yourself.

4. *Quiet* – is an integral part of this practice, in that it is solitary and doesn't involve verbal communication. This is a quieter opportunity to enter more deeply into the present moment. Note: it's okay that the moment isn't perfectly silent if you select music or a guided meditation. Both of these are pathways to getting quieter, when selected intentionally for this purpose.

Reflect

• What is it like to stop?

• As a parent, educator, or clinician, this might be a good time to explore your own reaction to stopping to pause, and take a break. We have values about staying busy leading to success, however, often slowing down helps us speed up later.

(19.) SELF-COMPASSION FOR PROCRASTINATION

Learn

At some point, teens procrastinate. The judgment, shaming, and criticism associated with procrastination can contribute to negative self-talk. Research demonstrates that procrastination is correlated with self-esteem, age, depression, and anxiety. Self-compassion practices show teens how to speak kindly to themselves when they are worried, feeling insecure, and/or helpless around tasks. They neutralize the negative effects of stress reducing the likelihood of depression, anxiety, and failure. See value in procrastination, as well as gain self-control to limit it. Here's how!

Practice

- Making friends with procrastination involves seeing the value in spending time on pleasurable activities and taking breaks.

- For some people, working with pressure associated with nearing deadlines promotes their best work.

- For others, there is a period of rest or waiting that precedes productivity.

- Regardless of the purpose of procrastination, it is a time to be honored and acknowledged.

Do you procrastinate?

_____

How often do you procrastinate?

_____

Is it a problem for you? (In other words, do you suffer consequences as a result of your procrastination?)

_____

Do you judge yourself for procrastinating? If so, how?

_____

Do you feel badly about yourself when you procrastinate?

_____

Are there any benefits to procrastinating? If so, list them.

_____

_____

_____

_____

_____

Reflect

- Procrastination serves a purpose.

- If you do something joyful while procrastinating, it is restorative. It recharges and rejuvenates. It also stimulates creativity and juices up the brain.

- The thing about procrastination is: It can control you if you don't control it.

- Set intentions and limits on procrastination. Be in charge of when and how you procrastinate by mindfully choosing what you do with your time.

- Remember to help teens see value in procrastination and find the benefits in it. It is an act of self-kindness to do so.

(20.) BULLYING

Learn

> "Bullies teach (all too often especially if they're adults in caregiver positions) self-loathing. . . Gentle/soft/coded/feminine is so humiliated and scorned that it makes kids believe the lie that compassion makes one vulnerable. To change that thinking to show the truth—compassion makes you powerful—will be so compelling."
>
> —Jennifer Fraser (Personal communication, January 4, 2016)

In *Teaching Bullies* Jennifer Fraser (2015) examines the bullying that teachers and coaches subject students to in the name of achievement. She tells the stories of fourteen students who spoke up about the harassment they consistently faced. There was a lot of social reprisal and traumatic legacy that followed. Much of it resonates with the dynamic Nancy Willard (Personal communication, February 10, 2016) found in her study of more than 1,500 US students, and their experiences being bullied. She explained that teens who bully tend to have strong social skills and many followers. This comes to them as a result of bullying to obtain dominant status, so followers tend to be silent bystanders, rather than active helpers when bullying occurs, in order to preserve their own social status and alliance with the bully. Willard suggested that one way to address this is by inspiring teen leaders who are kind and compassionate to speak up and/or privately report all instances of bullying. The following two self-compassion practices bolster teens who aspire to stand up to bullies, and also offer immediate and actionable resources for bullied teens, in the midst of being bullied.

Practice I: For the Bully and Bystanders

Self-compassion has four elements:

1. **Mindful awareness**

2. **Self-kindness**

3. **Shared humanity**

4. **The willingness to act to relieve one's own suffering**

- If you see someone bullied, or recognize yourself being a bully, congratulations on achieving the first and third aspects of self-compassion!

  - It takes mindfulness and strength to recognize suffering in someone else, and respect for common humanity and the interconnectedness of us all to realize that witnessing bullying hurts the witness just as much as the victim, and the bully. All three parties are hurting when any instance of bullying occurs.

  - Bullying may be a learned behavior, and also an aggressive reaction to a perceived threat.

  - When you see any bullying going on, you've just been exposed to violence. Being exposed to violence is a form of trauma, and it causes suffering.

- Self-kindness, especially the kind related to compassion, includes a willingness to act to relieve suffering.

- Commit now to being willing to speak up if someone is being bullied. Tell the bully to stop, if you can. Be kind to yourself if you can't. It's very hard to challenge a bully while they are bullying.

- Tell an adult in private if you witness bullying.

- If you realize you have bullied someone, please tell a trusted adult that you need help talking about difficult matters. There is help available, and you deserve it too! These last three bullets all cultivate the third part of self-compassion: self-kindness.

Practice II: For the Bullied Teen

- When you are being bullied, say to **yourself**:

"Even though I am afraid, and this is not okay, I can get through this."

- The mantra activates two aspects of self-compassion: **mindful awareness** of suffering in the moment, and **self-kindness**—giving yourself the encouragement and reassurance that you are okay and can get through difficulties.

- Avoid retaliating by enacting your safety plan.

- A safety plan includes the steps you take to keep yourself safe when threat is present. For example:

  o If you feel strong enough, tell the bully that you see he or she is hurting and wish the bully well. With kindness and firmness, say:

"Look, we see this differently, and I wish you well with your views."

  o It changes the whole game to focus on someone else's pain, different perspectives, and wish someone well. You're also reflecting a truth about common humanity and our interconnectedness: A bully who hurts others is also hurting. People who aren't in pain, don't hurt others. By feeling fear or pain at the hand of a bully, you get to feel what it's like to be the bully. The bully is generally the most afraid person in the room, and unwilling to admit it.

  o You can also invoke your "Declaration of YES and NO," stating that you decline to have the conversation at this time. It doesn't matter what the bully is saying, just decline to participate in the conversation, and leave.

  o If you are alone, and physically threatened, leave if you can. Find anyone else to assist you, and ask for help. It's okay to ask for help.

  o If you are with a friend, turn to your friend, and ask for help, and/or state the following:

"This person is hurting/stressed/angry/not feeling friendly/right, let's go!"
(Your friend may not know what to do either.)

Reflect

- Offer kindness and encourage self-kindness to the bully, bullied, and bystander teens for any and all reactions to the situation.

- If you are an adult caregiver, and know of any bullying going on, resolve to address it, and call in support from other adults, including experts in bullying and trauma.

- Giving teens permission and assistance to leave situations that include bullying is compassionate to them, and also teaches them how to say no to toxic relationships in the future.

5 Self-Compassion Training for Teens with Depression and Anxiety

There are three aspects of self-compassion:

1. **Mindful awareness**

2. **Self-kindness**

3. **Common humanity**

To these three I add the element of being willing to take action to relieve one's own suffering. This component of self-compassion is drawn from Stanford University's Center for Compassion and Altruism Research's working definition of compassion, which includes a bias to action. This bias to action is particularly impacted in teens suffering from depression and anxiety. Chapter 5 offers teachings, practices, guided meditations, and reflections to address the unique concerns of this population, with self-compassion.

(1.) GUIDED MEDITATION FOR DEPRESSION

Learn

Depression leads to isolation, loneliness, withdrawal, and negative thinking patterns. One way to disrupt these elements of depression is with meditations that connect teens to love and community. Love heals and purifies, while community offers the secret sauce that teens (as well as kids and adults) need as social creatures. The following meditation redirects teens' attention inward in a loving way, then outward as a benefactor to the world. This guided meditation becomes more impactful when practiced regularly, as one time isn't quite adequate for it to reduce symptoms of depression.

Practice

The following guided meditation can be spoken to your teen and/or recorded for listening alone later on. When the meditation is familiar to the teen, he or she can recall the various steps without guidance, and maintain it as a daily practice, if desired.

- Sit or lay down in a comfortable position.

- Close your eyes if it feels comfortable. If not, settle your gaze downward and fix it on a target.

- Settle into your body, feeling it touch the furniture you're seated on.

- Take a deep slow breath, all the way in to your belly.

- And slowly exhale through your mouth.

- Allow yourself to become present in this moment, in your body.

- Take another deep breath.

- This time feel the air enter your nose, fill your lungs and belly.

- And let it go.

- Take a third deep breath feeling the cleansing, energizing, healing, and purifying aspects of the air you take in.

- Allow your breath to travel deep into your belly.

- Slowly exhale.

- Take a moment to notice the ebb and flow pattern of your breath.

- *Give your teen about 45 to 60 seconds to breathe in and out in silence.*

- Imagine the flow of air entering your nose, traveling down to your belly, and out through your mouth is simultaneously creating a channel. In addition to the air that flows through this channel, pure white light infuses the channel and your whole being with a very special healing energy.

- Take a moment to notice the channel created by your breath, follow it with your attention and mind's eye.

- See the light flowing in the channel created by your breath.

- Every time you breathe in, imagine you are also taking in this pure white light, and silently say to yourself:

"I am love. And, I am peace."

- Allow yourself to enjoy this moment, your breath, and the healing light you're calling into your being.

- *Give your teen 45 to 60 seconds to enjoy the moment in silence, and deepen their attention in the mind's eye.*

- With your breath, direct the pure white light to cover every spec of your body, inside and out.

- Imagine the white light filling your whole being so that you become a glowing white being of light in your mind's eye.

- Silently say to yourself:

"I am love. And, I am peace."

- Now that your whole being is charged with pure white light, you can use your breath to share it with others.

- On your next breath, imagine the white light filling your heart area.

- Imagine your breath enters and exits at your heart space with every breath.

- When you exhale, move the white light directly out of your heart space through the chest wall.

- Imagine your heart is pushing the white light in and out of your chest, every time you inhale or exhale.

- Use your imagination to direct the white light to the room you are in, and watch the light fill the room.

- Move it to the whole building.

- See the whole building in your mind's eye.

- See it filled with white light, glowing and pulsing from the energy created by so much pure white light in one place.

- Every time you exhale and intentionally send the pure white light energy, it instantly goes wherever you intended.

- Your imagination is very powerful, and right now you're sharing healing power with the places you spend time in.

- When people come in contact with these places, they will be subtly affected by the healing properties of the pure white light you infused in that place, with your imagination.

- Send pure white light to your whole community.

- On the next inhale, imagine the white light filling your heart area.

- Silently say to yourself:

"I am love. And, I am peace."

- On the exhale, send the breath out of your heart through the chest wall propelling the pure white light to your whole suburb.

- See the light extend to the boundaries of your town.

- It's okay if you don't have a perfect map of your town in mind, just send the pure white light to the city limits, and set the intention for the light to spread and cover every single square inch of the suburb.

- Let every home, building, person, child, and pet be touched by the pure white light, even if they don't know it.

- See the whole town pulsating now as you've infused it with pure white light.

- On the next inhale, imagine the white light filling your heart area.

- Silently say to yourself:

"I am love. And, I am peace."

- On the exhale, send the breath out of your heart through the chest wall propelling the pure white light to your whole country.

- Notice the whole country full of pure white light, and trust wholeheartedly that you are gifting the whole country with a deeply needed healing elixir.

- If any bodies of water touch your country, breathe out pure white light into the water.

- Let all bodies of water that are interconnected receive and fill up with pure white light.

- See the whole planet Earth radiate with pure white light, as it spreads and touches everything and everyone.

- The pure white light absorbs all sadness.

- Let the world feel love and peace, let humanity be healed by the pure white light emanating from your heart.

- The world thanks you.

- Humanity thanks you.

- And, I thank you.

- Sit with this energy as long as you like.

- When you are ready to reenter the room, open your eyes and be gentle with yourself upon reentry.

- Namaste.

Reflect

- How did the pure white light affect you?

- Did you realize that while you are sad, you can still be a source of love and peace?

2. HORSESHOE MEDITATION FOR CLEARING ANXIETY AND DEPRESSION

Learn

The presence of anxiety or depression may signal stagnation. When teens ruminate, they get stuck in negative thinking, and can become depressed or anxious. When just stopping, and reframing in the positive direction is insufficient, teens can redirect energy at the level of imagination in order to kick-start the thinking process in another direction. The Horseshoe Meditation for Clearing Anxiety and Depression is a self-healing technique for the relief of symptoms associated with stagnant energy.

Practice I for Anxiety

- Direct your breath up into your right foot, into your right calf and hip, then along your right side and arm. Your breath is pulling the Earth's energy up your leg like a beverage through a straw.

- Watch the current of Earth's energy curve along your head with the flow of your breath.

- When the current of Earth energy reaches the crown of your head, use out breath, or exhale, to direct the anxiety/depression down and out.

- See the energy move down the left side of your face, neck, shoulder, and arm.

- Guide it down your left side past your left buttock, thigh, knee, and foot.

- Allow Earth's energy to transmit anything you do not need down to Her core.

- See the energy current instantly disappear into the center of the Earth where Mother Earth transforms it into energy that can be used by someone else.

- Repeat the horseshoe practice ten to twelve times.

Practice II for Depression

- The instructions for symptoms of depression are the same as for anxiety, however, the current of energy *begins with the left foot*, instead of the right, and *reverses* course.

Reflect

- Did you remember to breathe while imagining the current of energy running through your body?

- Connecting this practice with attention to your breath may take some time, however, your breath is like an amplifier that magnifies the effects of this practice.

- Over time, observe the energy that flows through the horseshoe. It will change as you do.

3. MOVING IN AND OUT OF THE DEFAULT NETWORK

Learn

The "default network" is a series of brain regions that are active when the mind is at rest. It is associated with free association, daydreaming, and creativity. Activity in this area of the brain can leave teens looking absentminded and inattentive, when they may be actively involved in creating personal meaning, planning, self-regulating, and even engaging in divergent thinking[3] (Kauffman, 2013). Training teens in self-compassion includes instructing them on the purpose and nature of this area of the brain, and giving them tools to move in and out of it, intentionally and purposefully. When teens get stuck in the default network for too long, it can lead to rumination, anxiety, and depression (Germer, 2009).

Practice

The purpose of this practice is simply to notice the difference between having an active mind and a wandering mind.

- Begin by placing your attention on your breath.

- Feel the cool air enter through your nose, and the warmth as it exits.

- Notice the rise and fall of your chest.

- Feel your belly inflate and deflate with every breath.

- When your mind wanders away from your breath, smile and acknowledge the default network is engaged.

- Continue this practice for a few minutes, remembering to smile every time your mind wanders away from your breath.

- Attach joy and amusement to the process of noticing your mind wander away from the target of your attention.

- Associating joy and amusement with the default network cultivates imagination and creativity, both of which heal with compassion to you, and all those you touch.

Reflect

- Have you ever been judged, or judged yourself, for having a wandering mind? If so, what are the judgments?

- It is very important to make friends with your wandering mind. Learning about the power and purpose of the default network is one way to do this.

- It is equally important to have mental control and not remain in the default network any longer than you intend and/or purposefully desire. Having the ability to set limits on this kind of thinking is very helpful in healing, creating, and relating to others.

---

3   Divergent thinking is defined by Kaufman (2013) as "the ability to come up with many different ideas, story themes, and symbols."

4. FLUSH DEPRESSION AND ANXIETY DOWN YOUR GROUNDING CORD

Learn

There are many ways to self-soothe when worried, sad, freaked out, or just down in the dumps. The following meditation practice eliminates the need for words to describe feelings or reasons for any experience of suffering. It offers instant access to the healing properties of imagination, while applying them to the reduction of symptoms associated with anxiety and depression. By associating uncomfortable feelings with color and moving the color out of one's being with imagination, teens become empowered in self-healing techniques. The ability to identify suffering and the willingness to engage self-healing approaches are both self-compassionate.

Practice

- Take a deep breath all the way into your belly.

- Feel your chest fall as the air leaves your body through your nose.

- Take two more centering breaths noticing contact with air at your nose, chest, and the bottom of your belly.

- Imagine there is a connector at the base of your tailbone.

- Examine the width and color of the connector, then attach a cord to it.

- See the cord drop down through the floor beneath you, magically and instantly penetrating the crust of the Earth and connecting to the core.

- The core of the Earth is a source of energy and a place where all energies can be transmuted into more useful forms of energy.

- When your grounding cord is connected to the Earth's core, you are "grounded." It's not the kind of grounding that happens when your parents put you on restriction. It's the centering kind, where you feel balanced, radical aliveness, engaged with life, and alert.

- Imagine the feelings you have right now as a color. Choose any color you like.

- With your intention and will, send the color out of your being down your grounding cord, into the Earth's core.

- Trust the feelings being sent to the core are being transmuted into useful energy and that you are in the process of letting them go.

Reflect

- How was it to flush your negative energy down your grounding cord?

- Is it believable that this can be useful? If your teen believes, it will work. If your teen does not believe in this practice, it will not work. Whatever you believe, you create.

5. BRAIN'S GROWING PAINS

Learn

According to Siegel (2013), the adolescent years may be the time when major psychiatric disorders become evident. This period is also characterized by emotional lability, and so discriminating between typical mood swings and those that require professional help can be tricky. Let this penetrate for a moment.

Practice

One way to begin discerning if moods are typical or not, is by sharing the following with your teen:

During the teen years, your brain goes through very intense changes. Brain connections formed in early childhood are trimmed so only the most relevant ones remain, and the irrelevant ones disappear. During this time, your brain can operate in rigid and chaotic ways, leaving your mind and interactions with others kind of wonky. Being kind with yourself when these times occur is one way to ease your brain's growing pains.

Reflect

- If your teen can reflect on this brain process, called '*pruning*,' and offer some self-kindness, the likelihood is that the moods are typical. If he or she cannot, there may be some internal disorganization and perceptual distortion operating, which would benefit from comprehensive evaluation and treatment.

- Teens can reflect on these moments of emotional dysregulation when they are not in the throes of emotion. If anxiety and/or depression are chronic, enduring, and unabating, they are less likely to be an example of the brain's growing pains.

- Which statements help your teen feel better when he or she is depressed/anxious?

- Help them create self-soothing statements to be used during times of distress.

- Some examples of self-soothing statements include:

"I am okay even though I don't feel okay."

"Feelings are real, but not true."

"These intense feelings are temporary; they always pass."

"Like good times, bad times come to an end."

"Everyone goes through moments like this; I am not the only one."

6. BREATHING PRACTICES FOR ANXIETY AND DEPRESSION

Cautionary Statement: The following breath practices are based on yogic pranayamas, and considered strong medicine with great power. Yoga principals teach us how to use energy, when to back off, and when to push forward. In the case of pranayamas, the urge to push forward can result in unexpected and intense reactions. As an adult caregiver of teens, please practice the pranayamas yourself, <u>before</u> introducing them to your teen. It is essential to know what the effects feel like to you, as you present them to teens. Furthermore, teens need to be guided in the pranayamas, and not left to practice alone. Try one pranayama at a time, and only for a little bit. Pay attention to the effects it has on your teen. If it is helpful, continue; if not, discontinue immediately.

Learn:

Invite your teen to lay down, recline, or settle into a relaxing position. Read this poem, by Mary Oliver, to your teen:

> *"Where Does the Dance Begin,*
> *Where Does It End?"*

Don't call this world adorable, or useful, that's not it.
It's frisky, and a theater for more than fair winds.
The eyelash of lightning is neither good nor evil.
The struck tree burns like a pillar of gold.

But the blue rain sinks, straight to the white
   feet of the trees
whose mouths open.
Doesn't the wind, turning in circles, invent the dance?
Haven't the flowers moved, slowly, across Asia, then Europe,
   until at last, now, they shine
     in your own yard?

Don't call this world an explanation, or even an education.

When the Sufi poet whirled, was he looking
outward, to the mountains so solidly there
in a white-capped ring, or was he looking

to the center of everything: the seed, the egg, the idea
that was also there,
beautiful as a thumb
curved and touching the finger, tenderly,
little love-ring,

as he whirled,
oh jug of breath,
in the garden of dust?

-from *Why I Wake Early by Mary Oliver*, published by Beacon Press, Boston Copyright © 2004 by Mary Oliver, Used herewith by permission of the Charlotte Sheedy Literary Agency, Inc.

Pranayama is the yogic practice of 'breath control.' *Prana* refers to the vital life force present in breath, while *yama* means control. Tapping into this vital life force, developing a relationship with it, and skills to control it, are associated with the relief of stress, depression, and anxiety.

Air is related to giving and receiving. It has no end and no beginning. Spending time with breath is a powerful means of connecting with oneself, increasing concentration, deepening mindful awareness, and creating self-kindness. The breath influences the nervous system, and can be used to manipulate states of consciousness. Breath practices teach us the skills for working with energy, shifting habitual patterns, and rewiring the brain.

Practice I for Anxiety

- Inhale for a count of 4.

- Exhale for a count of 6.

Practice II for Depression

- Inhale for a count of 6.

- Inhale for a count of 4.

Practice III: Balancing Anxiety with Breath

- Also known as **Nadi Shodhana,** alternate nostril breathing balances the life energy in the body and connects both sides of the brain.

- This practice calms the mind, while increasing energy and well-being, and decreasing depression.

- Sit comfortably with your head and spine erect and upright.

- Hold one nostril closed by gently pressing your thumb against the side of your nose.

- Breathe in a long slow breath, all the way into your belly, through the open nostril.

- Shift your thumb away from your nose, and allow your ring and pinky fingers to close the other nostril.

- Slowly exhale through the open nostril.

- Inhale back into the same open nostril.

- Cover the nostril you just breathed into with your thumb, and exhale through the other side.

- Keep going for several rounds.

- Notice the length of breath; play with it and see if you can control how evenly it flows in and out.

- See if you can balance the in breath and out breath to a count of 5.

Modification: For anxiety, inhale to a count of 5, and exhale for a count of 8.

Practice IV: Right Focused Breath for Depression

- Also known as **Surya Bheda**, right-nostril breathing is especially helpful for depression, weakness, lethargy, mental dullness, difficulty communicating, and withdrawal from the external world.

- Place your right hand in front of your face and cover your left nostril with the ring finger.

- Inhale slowly and deeply through your right nostril.

- At the end of the in-breath, close both nostrils, and hold your breath in.

- Gently lower your chin toward your chest, and gently tighten the perineum. This is the muscle of the pelvic floor—where you tighten when you have to go to the bathroom.

- Hold the breath for just a few seconds.

- Release the root lock, raise your chin up again, and exhale through the right nostril, while continuing to block the left nostril with your ring finger.

- Do this for only three rounds.

Practice V: Pushing Air

- Also known as **Bhastrika**, "Bellows Breath" is very useful for depression.

- Relax in a seated position.

- Close your eyes.

- Lengthen your spine.

- Take a few forceful and deep breaths in and out of both nostrils together.

- Pump your breath from the top of your belly where it meets your rib cage (diaphragm).

- Exaggerate the motion of your belly as you breathe in, growing it very big.

- Snap it back toward your spine when you exhale.

- Move right into the "Bellows Breath" by closing your right nostril with your right thumb.

- Breathe in and out forcefully through the left nostril 10 times, using only your diaphragm to move air in and out of your body.

- Keep your chest and shoulders still even while your breath is thrusting in and out.

- After ten breaths, inhale slowly and deeply through the left side.

- Hold this breath in, with both nostrils closed for a few seconds.

- Exhale through the left nostril.

- Repeat these same steps with the right nostril for ten breaths.

- Take a long breath in, and hold it for a few seconds.

- Exhale slowly, intentionally, and purposefully through the right nostril.

- Integrating the practice with both nostrils open now, breathe in and out forcefully for ten breaths.

- Start with slow breaths.

- Be gentle.

Practice VI: Darth Vader's Breath Practice

- Also known as **Ujjayi Pranayama**, "Victory Breath," "Ocean Breath," or "Psychic Breath" is excellent for relief of depression, anxiety, and stress.

- It soothes the nervous system, calms the mind, relaxes the body, relieves insomnia, and slows the heart rate.

- Breathe out through your nose while accentuating the sound of your breath at the back of your throat.

- When the glottis is constricted ever so slightly, it causes a deep throaty whisper sound as air passes by.

- This sound is audible to others, but not disruptive when practiced effectively.

- See if you can produce the whisper sound on the in-breath too.

Reflect

- Pranayama is powerful, and can lead to altered states of consciousness.

- Altered states are not dangerous, nor are they permanent, but they can be scary.

- Invite your teen to share her or his experiences with these breath practices.

- These practices don't have to be practiced regularly to be helpful, and therefore can be used on a one-off basis.

- Intensely focused Pranayama practice will have very extreme effects, and are therefore not encouraged for teens without guidance from a yogi.

- If any Pranayama exercises cause feelings of faintness, excessive sweating, or nausea, discontinue immediately and seek the guidance of a yoga teacher.

7. BREATHING PRACTICE FOR SLEEP

Learn

Sometimes the mind is too busy worrying and ruminating to sleep. Focusing on breath in very specific ways can lead to a calmer mind, and sleep induction.

Practice

- Inhale for a count of 4.

- Hold your breath for a count of 7.

- Slowly exhale over a count of 8.

Reflect

- Discuss and reflect on this practice for sleep compared to "counting sheep" or "counting bottles of beer on the wall."

- After sharing this practice, revisit with your teen later and see how it was for him or her to use this as a sleep aid.

8. CHANGE YOUR THOUGHTS AND BELIEFS TO REDIRECT YOUR LIFE

Learn

According to Gilbert (2009), it is harmful rather than motivational to have a self-critical inner dialogue. It leads to the negativity bias, which is a propensity for negative information and experiences to be encoded in memory, while positive ones drop off more easily. This tendency is linked to challenges in self-soothing and/or inadequate comforting in childhood (Germer, 2009).

The following practice is inspired by Kristin Neff's research (Germer, 2009), which suggests that self-compassion is associated with feeling connected with others, happiness, and the ability to self-soothe. Her data further suggest that self-compassion practices are not associated with depression, anxiety, rumination, and perfectionism. The premise behind "Change Your Thoughts and Beliefs to Redirect Your Life" is: When teens empty their minds of all the negative clutter, it creates space to fill with positive concepts. Judgments and beliefs can be self-sabotaging and self-limiting. Replacing harmful thoughts and beliefs with positive ones is not only an art, and a healing approach to depression and anxiety, but also the blueprint for creating reality. Every invention and innovation we now take for granted first started off as a mental image in someone's mind. Teens need to know their **thoughts create reality**. Filling the mental chatter space with positive ideas creates positive reality. Ruminating and obsessing over negative ideas and beliefs creates negative reality—a place where everything sucks!

Practice

Fill out the following worksheet.

Reflect

- Discuss with your teen: Were you able to suspend judgment and complete this task? Some people have a hard time letting go of their negative thoughts. They can't believe there is another way to think of things, so they don't. This task invites you to suspend judgment and disbelief, and just write things down.

- The act of bringing all the negative thoughts out, and putting them on paper is intended to release them from your mind space. Did you notice any clearing, anywhere in your body, or even just a little bit mentally?

- People tend to become attached to negative thoughts and beliefs due to faulty learning of associations or perceived self-protective features.

- The process of turning the negative thoughts into positive ones can be challenging if your teen is attached to their negative thoughts. It's okay. Invite your teen to write them down anyway, and then look at the column and see if any of the statements have evidence in reality. This is a key opportunity to guide teens, helping them remember proof of their goodness so they can cultivate the self-kindness component of self-compassion.

CHANGE YOUR THOUGHTS AND BELIEFS

- In the first column, list all the worries, stressors, fears, unmet needs, and negative beliefs you hold about yourself.

- Shift the negative idea into a positive one.

- You don't have to believe the ideas in the right-hand column, just write them there.

All negative thoughts	Transform into positive thoughts

- Notice what you wrote in the first column.

- For each one, put a number to the left of it, representing how true the negative thought is. For not true at all use 0 and use 10 for totally true. Choose any number that jumps out at you, even if you don't know why.

- Look at the right-hand column. Write down the number that corresponds to how true the statements are in that column to the right of each statement. Once again use the 0–10 scale, where 0 is not true at all, and 10 is totally true.

9. ANXIOUS ALIENS

Learn

Anxiety happens to everyone at some point. It can feel like being a live wire. For teens, it can arise when taking a test or giving a presentation on the mild end of the spectrum and increasing to school refusal or even panic attacks. Help your teen realize that we are all anxious aliens with varying degrees of anxiety arising at different times, for different reasons. (Practice 11 will demonstrate how anxiety is beneficial, but for now let's focus on the common humanity parts as well as how to keep it from interfering with functioning.) There are very real physical components to anxiety, and using mindful awareness techniques to notice these effects is a self-compassion practice.

Practice I: Remembering Common Humanity

- Anxiety can signal threat or harm, but usually it's a sign of something more emotional and less dangerous.

- It can happen when teens really want to be liked and/or accepted and think there is a chance that rejection will happen instead.

- Simply remembering the following statement when feelings of worry and nervousness arise can begin alleviating the suffering part of anxiety:

"Everyone gets anxious at some point. I am not the only anxious alien here."

Practice II: Accepting Anxiety

- Since anxiety can cause discomfort and suffering, it can be difficult to accept.

- Encourage teens to set the intention to accept anxiety whenever it is present.

- They can say silently to themselves:

"Hello Anxiety!"

- And then make a concerted effort to redirect attention to the task or activity at hand, if possible.

- This won't always be possible if:
  a. The task is the cause of anxiety.
  b. Trauma is at the root of anxiety.
  c. Anxiety is flooding and overwhelming.

- Discourage any analysis of the anxiety at this point.

- The goal here is to notice anxiety is present, and move on. That's all.

Practice III: Finding Anxiety in the Body

- This practice requires adult guidance in the beginning.

- Invite your teen to find a comfortable position, either lying down or seated.

- Say, "**Focus your attention on the top of your head, and move downward scanning your whole body. Your laser focus in this scan can pick up even the subtlest anxiety lying in your body. Notice if any part of your body feels tight or uncomfortable. As you notice anything in your body that bothers you, please tell me.**"

- As your teen relates parts of the body that are noticeably affected, log them here:

Part of the body	Describe the sensation	Intensity of the sensation (Rate it: 1–10 scale where 1 = low; 5 = medium; 10 = high)

- This is a two-person activity—the teen sits or lays comfortably while the adult logs the reports.

- Invite teens to rate the sensations on a 1–10 point Likert scale.

Reflect

- These three practices cultivate two different aspects of self-compassion: mindful awareness and common humanity. Discuss these aspects of self-compassion as they relate to anxiety.

- The self-kindness component of self-compassion is helpful in soothing anxiety. How might your teen develop kindness for her- or himself when feeling anxious?

- Invite your teen to make up soothing sentences they can use when feeling nervous or worried.

BEFRIEND STRESS AND REFRAME ANXIETY

Learn

Differentiating between anxiety and excitement can be just as challenging as working to improve a skill. Leveling up in life, or in a video game, entails harnessing resources and cultivating greater proficiency. In her 2013 TED Talk, *"How to Make Stress Your Friend,"* Kelly McGonigal explained that stress isn't necessarily bad for us. How we think about it is! Our body's reaction to coping with a challenge is very similar to anxiety. Yes, anxiety and being energized feel a lot alike, and are also similar to excitement and stress. If your heart is pounding and your breathing changes, it's because your brain needs more oxygen to perform at a higher level. This may be due to danger or a threat, but in most cases it isn't so. When people realize these bodily functions are helpful to performance, they tend to be less stressed and more secure in themselves. Let's remember, and impart to teens, that hearts also pound when we experience joy and love. Interpreting stress and nervousness as healthy is a self-compassion practice because it involves mindful awareness of the body's role in anxiety, as well as self-kindness in the face of the typical human experience of anxiety, stress, excitement, and growth.

In her book, *The Upside of Stress: Why Stress Is Good for You and How To Get Good at It*, Kelly McGonigal (2015) also suggested that stress causes people to seek out others. In doing so, the connection produces oxytocin, which alleviates the suffering associated with stress and anxiety. The third component of self-compassion, common humanity, is addressed when anxious teens are encouraged to seek out others for support. It contributes to changes at the biochemical level that produce relief from symptoms of anxiety and stress.

Practice

- The next time your heart is pounding from stress or anxiety, tell yourself:

> **"This is my body gearing up so I can rise to this challenge."**

Reflect

- The way teens think about things influences outcomes and their health too.

- Finding a positive spin on difficulties increases resilience.

- Discuss how thinking positively about stressful situations transforms us by moving agency from an external to internal locus of control.

- Explore how thoughts and beliefs impact biochemistry, health, and well-being.

11. FROM A FIXED MINDSET TO A GROWTH MINDSET

Learn

Stanford University psychologist Carol Dweck (2006) culled her research on college students into a book called *Mindset: The New Psychology of Success*, and distinguished between two mindsets. The *fixed mindset* prevailed in education, assessment, special needs, child development, and intellectual ability for decades. It proposes that one's abilities are fixed, and unchanging—usually based in genetics. This view prevailed before we understood the nature and extent of neuroplasticity. It held that intelligence and potential for success was largely genetic, and unchanging in adulthood once maturation and development concluded. People who continue to hold this mindset about themselves, or the teens in their lives, fail to thrive and achieve as well as those who hold a *growth mindset*, which embraces the potential for change and development, at any age. It is consistent with neuroimaging studies, and the human capacity to adapt when the brain is damaged.

For teens struggling with depression and anxiety, opening to a growth mindset, and releasing the constrictions of a fixed mindset, is an act of self-kindness. It relieves suffering to know you can change and grow and pull yourself out of a rut. When anxiety and/or depression are tied to feelings of helplessness and powerlessness, a fixed mindset may be operating with rigidity. According to Siegel (2013), rigidity is a sign of chaos in the brain. When teens understand the ever-changing nature of being human, adopting a growth mindset is easy. And, it also coincides nicely with the Buddha's concept of impermanence. Like everything, our skills and abilities are always changing. They won't always be developing, and once more advanced, they may not remain there as decline with age is inevitable.

Practice

Discuss these two different mindsets with your teen:

Fixed Mindset

• Fleeting and requires reestablishing your worthiness over and over again.

• The belief that your abilities are limited and predetermined.

• Possibly tied to an external locus of control.

Growth Mindset

• The genetics and nurturing we start off with in childhood are just a foundation upon which so many more skills and abilities are built.

• The personal qualities that define a person can be cultivated and changed over time by setting the intention to do so and applying the required effort.

• Everyone changes and grows with practice and experience.

• The growth mindset is consistent with the Buddhist concept of impermanence, and is a way to become comfortable with the ever-changing nature of being human.

- Change is inevitable. Growth is the degree to which you intentionally design and direct your personal development.

- It is more likely associated with an internal locus of control.

Reflect

- Do you see influences of growth/fixed mindset in your teen's life?

- How might you and your teen collaborate to promote a growth mindset?

- Please consider gamifying the growth mindset. Make a game of it, and ask your teen to create one with you. A playful approach to developing a growth mindset may result in faster and more joyful appreciation of a growth mindset everywhere.

(12.) SELF-REASSURING LETTER

Learn

According to Gilbert (2009), there are three affect regulation systems:

1. **Self-soothing**

2. **Drive**

3. **Threat analysis**

Transitioning from childhood to adulthood includes tending to soothing on one's own. By the teen years, parents are much less involved in this, however, teen distress levels are rising, which suggests self-soothing skills may be inadequate for coping, and for cultivating self-compassion. The goal of the self-soothing system is to promote a state of inner contentment and peace. When teens meditate, they can achieve states of inner calm, connectedness with others, and freedom from obsessive need seeking. Affection and kindness are known to produce oxytocin, the "cuddle chemical" or "love hormone." When teens are helped to offer kindness to themselves, they strengthen the self-soothing mechanisms in the brain.

The Self-Reassuring Letter is a practice that focuses on the first kind of affect regulation system: the self-soothing system. It invites teens to practice being kind to themselves, concerning an issue that is worrisome, depressing, and/or anxiety provoking. It specifically informs them of the value of self-soothing when cultivating self-compassion and/or coping with suffering.

Practice

• Settle into your chair, and say silently to yourself:

"I set the following intention freely of my own open heart, to write a reassuring letter to myself. I set the intention to be kind to myself, connect with my inner wisdom, and remember that I am one of many who suffer. These are my intentions set freely of my own volition and free will."

• Write yourself a letter.

• There is no right or wrong way to write this letter, nor is there a template.

• Allow yourself to open to whatever it is you need to hear, to feel reassured in your current situation of distress, worry, anxiety, or sadness.

• Write about the problems you face, then listening to the voice inside that knows exactly what you want to hear, write those words on the paper/screen.

• Here are three things you may wish to consider as you write this Self-Reassuring Letter:

1. Everyone suffers. Finding others to connect with when you feel down or worried is self-compassionate, healing, and one way to practice self-kindness.

2. Writing down your struggles is one way to start letting go of the pain that comes with them so you can face them with strength and courage.

3. Being kind to yourself is not a sign of weakness, selfishness, or self-indulgence. If you would help a friend in your own situation, it is even more important to help yourself. When you treat yourself at least as well as you treat your friends, you are practicing self-kindness. You don't have to believe you are worthy of your own kindness, just practice it. It rewires your brain so that happiness chemicals flow more often.

Reflect

- What was it like for your teen to write her- or himself a reassuring letter in a time of difficulty? Was it helpful? Hard?

- Did any resistance come up while writing the Self-Reassuring Letter?

- Was your teen able to connect with a kind inner voice that knows just what he or she needed to hear? Sometimes it is hard to find that inner voice. Remind them it is always there.

This practice is adapted from Kristin Neff, *Self-Compassion: The Proven Power of being Kind to Yourself* (New York: William Morrow, 2011) and Chris Germer, *The Mindful Path to Self-Compassion: Freeing Yourself from Destructive Thoughts and Emotions* (New York: Guilford Press, 2009.)

6 Self-Compassion Training for Teens with ADHD

> "It would be more logical to point out. . . that ideas and imaginative flights have bodily accompaniments, and that these need to be revered, and attended to, as well as ideas."
>
> —D. W. Winnicott

Teens facing attention and hyperactivity concerns represent a special population when training in self-compassion. The emphasis in self-compassion training for this group is placed on educating about the mind, how minds work in different ways, and people have different needs for moving about. Teens with ADHD who practice self-compassion also cultivate mindful awareness as a means of minimizing ADHD symptoms, and improving executive functioning. This involves learning about their bodies, as well as why they need to move and have thinking problems. Self-compassion practices also promote teens caring for themselves when feeling fidgety and needing to move. Paying attention to **body, mind, nutrition, activity, and attention** with self-compassion reduces the need for teens with ADHD to use medication.

Activities in this chapter address core areas of need for teens with ADD/ADHD, such as: body, mind, nutrition, physical activity, and attention.

(1.) I NEED TO MOVE RIGHT NOW!

Learn

Teens with ADHD may feel an impulse to move. This impulse can be intense and maddening, which is why youngsters with ADHD create havoc in classrooms. The self-compassionate approach to this element of ADHD first involves mindful awareness of, and respect for, the need to move. It is literally a need, like other human needs for water, air, and food. Though many of our needs are common, not all people share the same needs. Teens with ADHD have the unique drive to get moving. To honor this need, help teens find the times, places, and ways they can move their bodies so as to minimize the conflict associate with increased movement.

Practice I

Have your teen fill out the following worksheet to plan when to exercise.

Practice II

- Create opportunities for teens with ADHD to move vigorously and rapidly for 5 to 15 minutes.

- Hiking, running in place, and/or outdoors, biking, skipping, jump rope, and more cardiovascular exercises are excellent for this practice.

- Do it super fast and intense!

- Make a competition of it: See which of you can sustain a high intensity workout the longest.

Reflect

- Self-compassion arises when teens can mindfully determine their needs and suffering, engage self-kindness around challenges, and be willing to act to relieve pain and suffering. Being aware of movement needs and the increased hyperactivity and inattention that result when movement needs aren't met is step one to self-compassion for ADHD symptoms.

- The practice of self-compassion deepens when teens can prioritize their need to move, as much as they prioritize eating and going to school, for example.

- Self-compassion also involves remembering that others suffer too, in similar ways. For teens with ADHD, the universe of those who also suffer with inattention and/or hyperactivity is a lot smaller. This means they require even greater self-compassion to cope with and care for their symptoms.

- High intensity movement may help some teens with ADHD regulate and apply themselves to their tasks.

I NEED TO MOVE WORKSHEET

Practice I

When am I most fidgety and needing to move?

Morning _____%___

Afternoon _____%___

Evening _____%___

_____

TOTAL: 100%

Which movements feel the best to me?

_____

_____

_____

_____

_____

_____

How might I incorporate movement time into my daily routine?

_____

_____

_____

_____

2. ELEVEN ALTERNATIVE REASONS WHY TEENS HAVE ATTENTIONAL PROBLEMS

Learn

There are many reasons why teens have difficulty paying attention and remaining seated for extended periods of time. Some reasons are extrinsic, like schools operate in archaic ways that are not conducive to the very goals they try to achieve. We now know that sitting and listening to lecture-style teaching is one of the least effective ways to learn. Teens need to know that schools are essentially creating ADHD symptoms by upholding ancient pedagogical practices. Trauma, loss, and poverty are other external factors that can cause ADHD symptoms to appear. Internal causes of this same presentation can be attributed to processing difficulties at the sensory level, communication problems, and mood disorders too. Permission to acknowledge and discuss these truths is one way for teens to cultivate self-compassion around inattention and/or hyperactivity.

Practice

Review the list of causes of inattention and hyperactivity that follow. Put a checkmark next to those that might apply to your teen. It's okay if you don't know if one applies or doesn't—leave it blank or write *n/a*.

- ☐ Depression and sadness.
- ☐ Worry and anxiety.
- ☐ Learning difficulties.
- ☐ Mismatch between learning style and teaching approach.
- ☐ Sensory integration difficulties.
- ☐ Auditory processing problems.

- ☐ Speech and language difficulties; communication disorders can be receptive or expressive.
- ☐ Visual processing disorders.
- ☐ Trauma.
- ☐ Poverty.
- ☐ Loss.

Reflect

- Are any topics worthy of referral for evaluation? Could one of these be an unaddressed cause of inattention and/or hyperactivity masquerading as ADHD?

- Would your teen entertain reasons other than ADHD, as the cause of their inattention and hyperactivity?

- Would parents, teachers, and/or clinicians open a dialogue about your teen's inattention and/or hyperactivity that explores causes other than ADHD?

- Medications are inexpensive and fast-acting treatments. For this reason, they tend to be the first line of treatment for stubborn ailments. For ADHD, medication has offered great benefits and some side effects too. Alternative treatments that cost more money and take more time are often not considered, yet may be more compassionate and beneficial in the long run. Discuss this with your teen.

3. ADHD AND SENSORY INTEGRATION

Learn

Some experts believe ADHD is a regulation disorder, meaning it is hard for some people to regulate their attention and activity level. One suspected cause of this lies in sensory integration difficulties. First described in 1980 by A. Jean Ayres (2005), sensory integration is how the brain makes sense of information entering from all the senses. Ayres explored the proprioceptive and vestibular systems in addition to the five senses. Due to the physical component of ADHD, as well as the role of vision and hearing in learning, sensory integration approaches may be very helpful in managing symptoms. Most importantly though, they may provide much needed stimulation to the sensory system, which promotes regulation and a sense of well-being. Sensory integration therapies are provided by occupational therapists, and may serve as a way for teens with ADHD to learn self-compassion practices that are uniquely helpful to them.

Practice

- Consult an occupational therapist (OT) for activities that are therapeutic for teens with ADHD. Many can be conducted at home and in parks, not requiring a specialized sensory gym used by OT's.

- Create obstacle courses for teens that get them moving and rolling, twisting and turning about as they move through the course. The more ways they move their body, the more regulated they will be afterward.

Reflect

- Experiencing a sensory gym just one time can be a very influential way to coax teens with ADHD to acquire self-compassion practices uniquely suited to their neurology.

- The goal of this practice is to sensitize teens with ADHD, and their caregivers, to the therapeutic benefits of sensory integration activities on ADHD symptoms.

4. EXECUTIVE FUNCTIONING TRAINING FOR TRANSFORMING THE DEFAULT NETWORK AND MIND WANDERING INTO CREATIVITY

Learn

Kaufman (2013) described people with ADHD as having increased mind wandering, and difficulty suppressing the default network as tasks get harder. He also stated that people with ADHD have greater tendencies toward divergent thinking and creativity, both of which are responsible for inventions, innovation, and artistic creations. In other words, people with ADHD are often responsible for some of the greatest discoveries and breakthroughs. Kaufman suggests that teens with inattention "may just require a little executive functioning training to get on a path to creative greatness!" The following practice aims to introduce teens with ADHD to the default network (Chapter 5) in the brain, and how to harness it for peak performance.

Practice

Executive functioning has four components:

1. Goal setting.

2. Planning and carrying out actions required to meet the goal.

3. Self-monitoring while carrying out the plan; evaluating the efficacy of the plan.

4. Willingness to adjust the plan as needed to achieve goals.

   - Teach teens about this aspect of being human.

   - Discuss how it is for your teen to set goals, implement plans, take and sustain action while monitoring the progress toward the goal.

Reflect

- Awareness of executive functioning and related strategies is one way for teens with ADHD to strengthen attention and rewire their brains.

- Helping teens cultivate healthy executive functioning habits are foundational to creativity too.

- Explore your teen's creative interests and abilities.

- Nurture creativity, talent, and interests to channel ADHD in a productive area.

5. THE MILLENNIAL NEURODIVERSITY REVOLUTION

Learn

Neurodiversity is a term coined by Judy Singer, herself a sociologist with high-functioning autism, whose own child also has high-functioning autism. The term brings compassion and kindness to those with different neurological makeups. Just as our thumbprints and genetic codes are unique, so too are our intellectual, attentional, creative, perceptual, and neuronal profiles and structures. When teens receive a diagnosis to explain these natural human variations, it causes suffering. The neurodiversity movement brings compassion to those who experience the world differently. Teens with ADHD are among those including themselves in the movement, and driving others to see the benefits of thinking and behaving differently.

Practice

- When thinking about the effects ADHD has on your life, try to see if any are positive. Please describe them here:

  _____

  _____

  _____

- There are many different ways to contribute to the world, your community, your family, and your group of friends. What are your unique contributions to any of these groups?

  _____

  _____

  _____

- What would it be like to rethink ADHD as a human variation that has value for evolution and survival of our species? Please imagine and describe what type of evolution needs to occur that teens with ADHD may already be highly skilled in:

  _____

  _____

  _____

Reflect

- Self-acceptance is a form of self-kindness that promotes relief of pain and suffering.
- Learning that one's behaviors are unacceptable, and worse pathological, is in itself painful for teens and their families.
- The goal of the neurodiversity movement is to promote inclusion and acceptance of those who are different.
- Find the benefits to ADHD.

6. NUTRITION AND ADHD

Learn

Some teens feel more wired after eating and drinking certain foods or beverages. Others get a foggy, cloudy head from consuming particular foods or drinks. A self-compassionate approach to nutrition and ADHD involves becoming mindful about the effects foods have on your teen. Many people habituate to harmful chemicals in their food sources, and don't notice they are impacted by those foods. The following practice engages awareness about which foods support feeling healthy and well, and those that make it hard to think and fidgety all over. What may work for one teen, may not be relevant for another one.

Practice

Keep a food log (template on the next page) for three to seven days.

Reflect

- Review the log with your teen.

- Help her or him to eliminate foods that contribute to concentration problems and/or hyperactivity.

- Invite your teen to consider trying new foods, wholesome organic foods, especially. Observe, log, and track the effects these new foods have on concentration and activity level.

- Consider watching food documentaries together to learn more about the impact food has on people.

- Help your teen see that eating healthy food is a self-compassionate practice because it is kind, and has the potential to heal.

- Mindful awareness about the impact food has on teen bodies is beneficial for most, yet possibly helpful in reducing symptoms associated with ADHD.

FOOD LOG

Date	Time	Food or drink consumed	How did you feel immediately afterward?	How did you feel 3 hours later?	Was there any impact on your concentration or activity level?

7. WATCHING THOUGHTS

Learn

Following the lead of the neurodiversity movement, teens benefit from spending quiet time with their thoughts. It helps them get acquainted with the noise in their mind, honors their unique flow of mental images and sounds, and respects the potential for creativity lying in wait. For teens with ADHD, the opportunity to observe the mind cultivates attention, disciplined thought management, impulse control, and more. The more practice with this type of meditation, the more neuronal connections develop to support sustained attention. Essentially, meditation is effective in cultivating attention.

The following practice is a formal experience aimed at pausing and learning about the richness that exists in active teen minds. For teens with symptoms of ADHD, this practice is an appointment with themselves to attend to the stuff that normally pulls their attention away from other, equally important yet less interesting tasks.

Practice

Offer these instructions orally, or record:

- Settle into yourself; feel your body make contact with the furniture, and feel your feet on the floor or wiggle your toes.

- Take a deep breath all the way down into your belly. Allow your breath to fill your lungs and your belly, then hold it for a count of three.

- Exhale through your mouth.

- Repeat this deep breath pattern two more times.

- Imagine a cord connected to you at your tailbone. See the cord travel through the Earth's crust, all the way down the central core of Mother Earth.

- This is your grounding cord. Notice the color and width. The qualities and dimensions of the cord will change over time. Every time you sit down to meditate, look at your grounding cord.

  You can disconnect it in your imagination, allow it to drop down to the center of the Earth, where it instantly disappears.

- Your grounding core travels to the center of the Earth without any effort at all, only your imagination and intention are needed to use it and replace it.

- Feel free to give yourself a new grounding cord whenever you like, and every time you meditate.

- For the next few minutes, simply observe your thoughts and feelings as they float by.

- Once you notice the thought or feeling, allow it to pass.

- If you notice yourself getting caught up in a thought or feeling, which isn't passing, return your attention to your breath for a moment and take a deep breath with the intention to express the thought or feeling through your grounding cord, on the exhale.

- Allow the ideas and feelings to float away even if they seem really compelling or interesting. When you let them go, you're practicing surrender, which means that you trust your best ideas and most important feelings will come again.

- During this practice, your goal is to get to know your inner thoughts and feelings and let them go. That's it!

- You can do whatever you like with them when your time to watch your thoughts is over.

Reflect

- The goal of this practice is to observe and allow thoughts to pass.

- ADHD is associated with inattention or distractibility. Perhaps the inner world is more compelling than the outer world.

- Empowering teens with symptoms of ADHD to take time for watching their thoughts essentially trains them to honor themselves.

- Some thoughts, ideas, or emotions may seem very important or interesting. The goal is to notice the idea, thought, or emotion, and let it go. Trust that it will arise in your mind again if it is truly worth more of your time.

- The more a thought, idea, or emotion arises, the more likely it is to need expression, outlet, or release. Help teens identify which ideas to let go of, and which to pursue further. This type of discrimination in thinking patterns also improves executive functioning.

8.) SELF-MANAGEMENT

Learn

According to Garland (2014), self-management is the behavioral practice of placing responsibility for managing behavior and attention on youngsters. This practice is critical for cultivating independence, especially for teens with ADHD and/or executive functioning challenges. It is consistent with the cultivation of self-compassion because it promotes teens self-reflecting and mindfully appraising themselves. Combining self-management behavioral programs with self-kindness and intentional actions on the part of teens contributes to the relief of their own suffering.

Practice

- Self-directed learning is perhaps the single greatest example of self-management programs that arise organically.

- Consider inviting your teen to create their very own learning programs.

- Start small. It's okay if the result is small or even if hardly anything emerges from the effort.

- The key is to engage your teen in starting projects that interest them, and allowing them the freedom to create and enjoy them, or see themselves not meet their own expectations.

Reflect

- The act of initiating any program for oneself is a self-compassion practice because it sets in motion patterns, habits, and behaviors that are useful for relieving one's own suffering.

- In the case of teens with ADHD, this practice initiates the development of self-organizing/ regulating/directing skills. It also promotes sustained attention while capitalizing on teens' organic interests and desires.

- Teens with ADHD who are unlikely to complete self-directed learning projects create rich opportunities to practice self-compassion. Mindful awareness of not meeting one's own needs and expectations, combined with kind self-talk, can ease moments of failure (see Chapter 4 for more on celebrating FAILURE).

(9.) FREEDOM TO LEARN

Learn

In his 2013 book, *Free to Learn*, Peter Gray lays out the science and research behind democratic educational practices. He explains how giving youngsters freedom to play and explore their own interests is not only effective pedagogy, but better suited to their natural instincts.

For teens with ADHD, this concept may be even more relevant, and compassionate, than any practice presented thus far and/or medication. Traditional classrooms are appropriate for a certain kind of student. Teens with ADHD are naturally more impulsive and fidgety than others, making them a very poor fit for the traditional classroom. Rather than adapting this type of student to educational settings that aren't a good fit, education reform is looking at how to meet these students where they are.

Instead of directly managing attention and hyperactivity issues with medication, think about creative, alternative, and innovative educational settings. The use of stimulant medication for attention and hyperactivity concerns evolved out of compassion for students, teachers, and parents, however, it misses the mark for self-compassion. Democratic schools, for example, literally eliminate some causes of inattention and hyperactivity by respecting teens' interests, drives, passion, and curiosity. Honoring their uniqueness and allowing students to set their own learning paths are key ways to give them space to be self-compassionate. Teens with ADHD may need freedom to learn more than most teens, precisely because the format normalizes, respects, and embraces their natural tendency to explore. Teens who embrace democratic learning practices simultaneously train in self-directed learning. The ability to learn anything on one's own is a self-compassion practice, especially with the Internet as an infinite home of open source educational content and MOOC's. For teens with ADHD, the ability to self-direct learning removes the great burden of fitting into outdated school paradigms. Teens with ADHD may be demonstrating how mismatched their educational setting is to their unique needs.

Practice

- Are there any democratic schools (also called Sudbury Valley Schools) in your area? Seek them out and visit them with your teen. See if they may be a better fit than the current school.

- If there aren't any democratic schools in your area, consult a professional in your teen's school or community to see if self-directed learning opportunities are available. Even if this becomes an extracurricular activity, it holds great value for college applications (if appropriate and desired), bolstering executive functioning skills along the way.

- Also consider alternative schools, and those pushing the envelope with innovative curricula and learning approaches. The more out of the box, the better!

Reflect

- Discuss what it would be like to go to a school where students are free and respected as equal members of their school community.

- Explore the concept of freedom and how complying with school rules may influence ADHD symptoms.

- Self-compassionate teens take action to reduce their symptoms of inattention and hyperactivity. One way of doing so is by finding learning environments that are suited to their unique way of seeing and experiencing the world. Freedom, self-directed learning, and responsibility to a community address the attention and activity needs of teens with ADHD.

7 Self-Compassion Training for Teens with Body Image Concerns and Eating Disorders

The media sensationalizes unrealistic body and image standards for both males and females, while the food industry seduces youngsters with more immediate options than ever before. Combining these messages, and abundant food options, with maturing bodies, and teens are subject to the perfect storm when it comes to their relationship to their bodies and food. This chapter illustrates the contradiction between healthy values and those promoted in school cafeterias and the media, while offering self-compassion practices teens can use to overcome behaviors and values that may be personally toxic to them.

1. SELF-HARM/CUTTING: A BODY NEEDING SELF-COMPASSION

Learn

According to Jennifer Fraser, "Self-harm/cutting is an inarticulate teen way of seeking compassion from the exterior body, without realizing it lies within . . . It is the difference between the danger of extrinsic motivation versus so much healthier intrinsic motivation." Fraser was tapping into deep wisdom when she connected cutting to the faulty search for self-compassion. She understands the neurobiology involving cascades of endorphins when teens cut, and how maladaptive that way of coping truly is. Moreover, she notices that self-compassion comes from a deeper place than the one where endorphins flow, and that it takes internal motivation to cultivate it.

When teens are cutting, their body has become the arena for both harm and relief. For this reason, this chapter begins with the prompt to observe and/or assess your teen for any signs and symptoms of self-harm, *in addition to eating and body image problems*. They are related because of the shared focus on the body as the source of defect and ultimate salvation. The first self-compassion practice offered here is *only* for teens who are self-harming and experiencing eating and body image concerns. Due to the seriousness of this combination, it is strongly recommended that teens with this presentation be referred for treatment by a licensed mental health professional, if not already in treatment. It is likely that they also suffer from trauma and/or other buried problems.

Practice

- Explore the benefits of cutting.

- Discuss the various methods of harming the body, with special focus on more subtle forms of harm like restricting food intake, binging, and using laxatives/diuretics/drugs.

- Pay special attention to long-term damage that arises from eating disorders, such as damage to teeth from purging.

- The purpose of this discussion is to help your teen become mindful of the impact their self-harm practices have on them.

- Bringing this topic out into the light is one way of decreasing shame and promoting recovery. It requires great care and the kindest, nonjudgmental approach as these teens are already hurting themselves and can easily turn to self-harming if they feel they are in danger.

- There is no goal of this practice, nor does it need to be repeated or sustained.

- This practice is intended as a crucial warning to adult caregivers of teens who have eating and body image disorder and also cutting. It is intended to sensitize all parties to the harm arising as a result of teen suffering.

Reflect

- Seek out a licensed mental health support for this teen.

- If you are a mental health clinician, please consider the level of pain and suffering this teen is experiencing, and consider some case management options to reduce the level of the teen's suffering.

- Residential treatment may be the most impactful and safest act of compassion, given the potency of this combination.

(2.) MINDFUL EATING: 50 CHEWS

Learn

Overeating is a significant problem in the United States. With restaurant portions large enough to feed multiple people, self-disciplined eating is also a self-compassion practice. Setting the intention to eat portions that are satisfying, without overeating is one step. 50 Chews is a self-compassion practice designed to connect teens with the physical sensations of eating, in order to cultivate increased mindful awareness. It takes time for the abdomen to register satiation, send the signal to the brain, and then for teens to notice they are either full, or getting full. Pausing to wait for the brain to receive signals of fullness from the belly is an essential self-compassion practice for teens who overeat. It creates mindful awareness about the body's signals, while training in healthy eating habits.

Practice I

- When eating, count each chew of food and see if you can get to 50 chews.

- Sometimes your food will be all gone before you get to 30!

- For fun, create a personal challenge to see what the greatest number of chews is that you can count, before your food dissolves.

- While counting chews, concentrate on the sensation of the food in your mouth. Truly notice the taste and texture.

- When you swallow, pause and silently count to three.

Reflect

- This can be practiced alone, or with others.

- Discuss the sensations you noticed when you ate mindfully.

- Explore how complex eating is, how much the body goes through to break down food, and how much more work is involved when teens overeat. The goal is to sensitize them to the suffering they cause themselves when they overeat, not only in belly discomfort, but also at deeper levels of body operations.

③ <u>SELF-FORGIVENESS FOR OVEREATING</u>

Learn

Overeating is associated with feeding to feel better. The pleasurable sensations that arise when eating are a maladaptive form of coping that contributes to obesity. It's a vicious cycle fueled by self-hatred and also results in more self-disgust. Self-forgiveness is a component of self-compassion for overeating because it evokes self-kindness when and how it is most needed.

Practice

- Encourage your teen to speak kindly and lovingly to themselves when they overeat.

- Words of love include:

"It's okay that you overate. You'll feel better soon."
"I forgive myself for exceeding the food quantity I know I need."

- Encourage your teen to repeat the words out loud several times and/or write them down on paper five to ten times.

- The reason for saying this out loud and/or writing it several times on paper is to take it from the mental plane to the physical plane, thereby giving it more power in the plane of positive reality.

Reflect

- How is it to offer yourself forgiveness when you've messed up?

- Are there any barriers to forgiving yourself?

- Could you see yourself applying this practice to any other ways you are unkind to yourself?

4. VISIONING FOR A HEALTHY BODY

Learn

The cultural messages about bodies dominate the media and are highly policed. Meaning, bodies that don't conform to standards of beauty are vilified, rejected, harmed, and discriminated against. To counteract this problem requires great inner strength. To begin teens along their journey of healthy body self-acceptance, the following practice is offered as a means of exploring bodies. This practice is appropriate for males and females.

Materials needed:

- Magazines

- Bristol board

- Scissors

- Glue

- Markers

Practice

- Invite your teen to cut out images of bodies.

- The only prompt to offer is for your teen to collect as many different images of the gender they select.

- The goal is not to find the ones your teen likes best or least, but rather to find the widest range.

- Images in magazines will likely be highly desirable according to societal norms.

- Encourage your teen to look elsewhere to find other bodies of the gender they chose.

- Help them find bodies that are nonconventional and set in a favorable context. (Dove Soap campaigns featuring women of all sizes, along with Matt Blum's Nu Project book series, are two options to explore with female teens. And disabled models and athletes represent a unique category to explore with male teens.)

Reflect

- This is a one-off practice that doesn't require repetition to be effective.

- It is offered as a means of opening a dialogue about the full range of bodies, and encouraging teens to see theirs with loving kindness, no matter what the size or shape.

5. HONORING MY BODY

Learn

Self-compassion practices promote self-kindness. When it comes to the internal dialogue people have with their bodies, the highest level of self-kindness is beneficial. The following practices are all intended to spark a positive, friendly dialogue and inner relationship.

Practice I

This practice focuses on the magic of the body, and how integral it is to our daily functioning. Remembering to be grateful for a functioning body is one way of sustaining health and creating a positive relationship between teens and their changing bodies.

- Invite your teen to use the following statement to speak kindly to themselves about their bodies:

    "I am grateful I was born and get to have this unique life experience being me, in this body."

- It's okay if the statement is not believable at this moment. It is intended to initiate a positive response to one's body.

- When you repeat positive statements in the mind, the brain wires itself along those lines, and begins creating life patterns to reflect the statement. The mind wants to be right all the time—tell it to do right and right it will do!

Practice II

Mindful body is one aspect of developing self-compassion regarding body image and eating disorders. Mindful body means mindfully connecting your teen with their body, and teaching them to continue to nurture this connection. Here are some statements your teen can use to cultivate mindful body:

> **"I take great care of my body."**
> **"I take good care of myself."**
> **"I feel centered in my love and gratitude for my body."**

- It's okay if these statements aren't true yet. The goal is to set the path of thinking mindfully and lovingly about the body.

Practice III

The body is a source of great wisdom. It knows what it needs, and if your teen listens and pays attention to the signals, she or he can know too. This simple practice is wonderful for becoming mindful about needs so they can be met.

- Invite your teen to close their eyes.

- Take two deep breaths all the way down into the belly, and exhale through the mouth.

- Now tell your teen to silently ask themselves:

"Body, what do you truly need right now?"

- The response that first comes to mind may be all the information your teen needs. However, sometimes the first thing that comes to mind isn't always healthy, such as ice cream, for example. When this happens, there are two options:

   a. Go with it, and eat or do the thing that is unhealthy. This can be self-compassionate when the net result is joyful, and nonharming. Eating a little ice cream can create joy, while eating a quart may not. Choosing to eat or do the unhealthy idea is one way of training in being kind to oneself, and finding the approaches that work and don't work.

   b. The second option to "hearing" something unhealthy, is simply to tell your teen to ask the body again.

Practice IV

- Feeling centered and grounded in the body is integral to healthy eating and body image.

- To center and ground, practice Body Scan with Grounding from Chapter 3, Practice 2.

- When the practice is well-established, teens can use the following command to instantly ground themselves:

"I feel centered in my body."

- The command acts as a silent verbal cue from your teen to his or her mind, and creates the grounding necessary for a healthy relationship with the body.

Practice IV

The body is defined by boundaries and a perimeter uniquely its own. Creating a healthy body image from a self-compassion practice involves being kind to oneself. One way of being kind to oneself and declaring an unwillingness to suffer unnecessarily is by setting boundaries (see "Declaring YES and NO! in Chapter 4) This is crucial where body image and eating disorders are concerned. According to Elisha Goldstein in *The Now Effect* (2012), a study examining the effect of social groups on obesity found a causal relationship. Obesity isn't shared only among immediate friends and family, it is "contagious" by up to three degrees of separation. The habits of the people around your teen affect your teen. Setting boundaries around people that have unhealthy habits is an act of self-compassion because it promotes health in multiple ways.

- Here is a statement to encourage your teen to remember this is part of developing a healthy body:

"I take good care of myself; I set boundaries when and wherever necessary."

Reflect

- You can use the statements and commands listed previously as often or as little as feels right to your teen.

- The more they repeat the statements or actions, the more impactful they will be.

6. SELF-COMPASSIONATE FOOD TRIGGER INVENTORY

Learn

When people are struggling with food concerns, journaling is one way of increasing mindfulness about eating. Many overeaters associate food with self-care, nurturing, and soothing. Overeaters can use food as a coping mechanism, and as such figuring out the triggers can reduce the need to use food for coping.

Practice

Fill out the log as a means of identifying patterns in eating.

Date	Time	What happened right before you ate?	What did you eat? Why?	What happened afterward?

Reflect

• Self-kindness around overeating can occur when teens are helped to see it as an attempt of coping with difficulties.

• More self-kindness arises when teens find healthy habits to replace overeating when they are in distress.

• This worksheet is intended to help teens and their adult caregivers become mindful and kind about overeating.

⑦ LETTING GO FOR SELF-LOVE

Learn

Paul Gilbert, author of *The Compassionate Mind* (2009), explains the etiology of eating disorders stemming from "threat emotions of anger, anxiety, and/or disgust" with the self. The pursuit of ideal body image through diet and exercise, he says, is like an addiction that gets fueled by positive results. The "addicted" end up devastated when they lose control and gain weight. Gilbert describes the self-criticism and self-hatred that arise with eating disorders and are associated with a lack of self-kindness or even loving allowance. Gilbert identifies the drive, need, preoccupation, and fear that make up the cycle of eating disorders. Coupled with feelings of powerlessness and helplessness, eating disorders can represent a maladaptive effort of people trying to control and correct their lives.

Practice

- Let go.

- The practice instructions are simply to let go.

- Anytime something arises that you can let go, do so, and notice that you let go.

Reflect

- This practice initiates the flow of letting go so that your teen can reduce or eliminate the strong attachment to body ideals and maladaptive habits.

 # Self-Compassion Training for Traumatized Teens

> "Self-compassion contains all the healing properties of mindfulness practice—awareness of present experience, with acceptance—but its truly unique character comes out when dealing with intense and disturbing emotions."
> —Christopher Germer, 2009

While training in self-compassion helps traumatized teens, the practice can be further traumatizing and, therefore, requires sensitivity and precautions. Mindfulness is one component of self-compassion, and for traumatized teens, tuning into the present moment can lead to awareness of triggers and flooding of emotion. Christopher Germer (2009) describes the first stage of developing self-compassion as the "backdraft" because the practice gives "oxygen," attention, and awareness to suffering that was previously deprived of "oxygen." **The effects of initiating self-compassion in the face of traumatic suffering can be flooding and lead to decompensation, and/or even dissociation.** To protect against this, while promoting healing, teens that suffered trauma benefit from different types of practices and instructions when beginning to cultivate self-compassion. The *Self-Compassion Training Protocol for Traumatized Teens* is offered to mitigate the risks.

(1.) THE SELF-COMPASSION TRAINING PROTOCOL FOR TRAUMATIZED TEENS

Learn

The Self-Compassion Training Protocol for Traumatized Teens is offered for this specialized population, with a focus on mitigating the risks of decompensation and dissociation. Traumatized teens need to be prepared and grounded with safety practices when beginning to train in self-compassion. The risks of overwhelming emotions of despair, helplessness, powerlessness, rage, terror, vulnerability, and loss emerging as a result of self-compassion practices are great, and traumatized teens need to be prepared for this possibility. Self-compassion isn't only about speaking kindly to oneself and minimizing self-criticism, it is also about getting clear about suffering and its causes, so a person can take action to relieve his or her own suffering. For traumatized teens, this is more crucial because their suffering tends to be so great it can be partially or completely dissociated.

Practice: Self-Compassion Training Protocol for Traumatized Teens

1. **Trust and depth in relationship with clinician**
   - Because self-compassion involves contact with pain and suffering, traumatized teens require special support to face their hurt.

   - This protocol begins with the relationship between a traumatized teen and her or his therapist because that relationship is the bedrock to cultivating a stable and healing self-compassion practice.

   - The therapist must have a consistent self-compassion practice, in order to help traumatized teens cultivate one.

   - A therapeutic alliance that is less than solid could further injure traumatized teens and as such is contraindicated for beginning self-compassion training with traumatized teens.

   - To deepen trust and rapport, therapists are encouraged to be more available to traumatized teens than with typical patients.

   - Traumatized teens who can rely on their therapist for support between sessions while training in self-compassion can be aided through the healing process with more ease and comfort than if left to practice alone without support.

2. **Centering and grounding**
   - Centering and grounding practices previously mentioned in Chapter 3, are effective in helping traumatized teens gain the emotional and mental footing needed to explore pain and suffering.

   - The grounding cord can be examined and replaced at any moment for any reason. Simply doing so creates a ground to the center of the Earth, as in an electrical ground that prevents user contact with high voltage and limits the accumulation of static electricity.

   - Emotional and spiritual grounding keeps individuals firmly rooted in the Earth, so that emotions, ideas, beliefs, and even external influences don't bombard and knock them over.

- When overwhelmed, traumatized teens may also use music to anchor them in the present moment (Germer, 2009) and reorient to something soothing and enjoyable. Gazing at an object, a beloved pet, or even a roaring fire are also good ways to anchor attention and become centered again.

3. Deep body breathing

- Instruct teens to breathe deeply into their belly three times.

- Direct them to hold their breath at the top of the inhale for a count of 5.

- And then, exhale slowly and purposefully through the mouth.

- With the exhale, imagine all pain, suffering, negative energy, ideas, beliefs, and memories flow out and away.

- Trust that Mother Earth will take it all from you, transmute it, and return it to the universe where it can be better used by someone else.

- The more often you practice this, the more effective it becomes.

4. Build positive and negative affect tolerance

- Teens who have been traumatized have a difficult time tolerating negative affect, and believing that positive affect is real, possible, and safe for them.

- To counteract this problem, traumatized teens and their adult caregivers can collaborate to create opportunities to increase affect tolerance in both directions.

- For negative affect, begin with scaffolding and serve as the support your teen needs, when they need it. Traumatized teens don't need to be in acute crisis to warrant a chat with their therapist between sessions because of the pain they have already been exposed to. This is a unique quality to treating traumatized teens, and therefore clinicians are invited to increase their availability between sessions for this reason.

- Adjunct treatment with EMDR, or other trauma treatments with integrated somatic and mindfulness components, is recommended to desensitize triggers and traumas, as well as to increase affect tolerance in both directions.

- For positive affect tolerance, invite teens to share or write down any positive feelings they experience. This can be an ongoing journal activity, for one week only, or a verbal report in session. Let your teen choose the span that feels right.

5. Define and explore abreaction

- According to Shapiro (2001), abreaction is "the re-experiencing of the stimulated memory at a high level of disturbance."

- Abreaction can happen at any time, and be stimulated by a trigger associated with a traumatic memory.

- It is a serious event, which involves a great deal of terror for traumatized teens. It is a time when orientation can be compromised, and the reminder that your teen is safe in the present moment is needed most.

- Explain to teens that self-compassion practices involve touching pain and suffering, which can cause them to have intense levels of disturbance that are very confusing and powerfully energizing in a negative way.
- Preparing teens and creating an understanding with them about how to cope with abreaction, when and if it occurs, is crucial to the success of treating traumatized teens and also in cultivating a sustainable self-compassion practice.

6. **Set expectations: The feelings will be real, but not true, and they should be treated as *reexperiencing* rather than *experiencing for real.***
   - According to Rinpoche and Swanson (2012), feelings are real, but they are not true. They explain that feelings can be strong and we feel them as if they are wholly real, in the here and now, but they aren't always true.
   - Take fear for example, when truly in danger, people rarely feel fear because they are mobilized to protect themselves from danger. When we feel fear, it is a real feeling, but it isn't necessarily true that we are in danger and know what to be afraid of.
   - Traumatized teens who remember this about their feelings can begin increasing toleration as they reengage rational thinking, and disengage the amygdala.

7. **Allow emotions to flow through you, and out for complete release**
   - Just as crying can be reframed as a cleansing process, feelings can move through for the purpose of release.
   - When purpose and meaning are added to situations, they take on new significance, and the perception of suffering decreases.
   - Having an emotion can signify letting go, which is a normal aspect of healing.
   - When a cut heals in the skin, a scab forms. Over time, the scab sloughs off. Sometimes, a new scab emerges, and at other times, the wound is open for a while and then heals. Emotions are like the scab forming and falling off.
   - Permission to feel emotions, and appreciate their purpose in the healing process, gives meaning to suffering, which also eases it.

8. **Breathe through and with pain**
   - Women laboring to deliver babies are directed to breathe through contractions. Likewise, life is full of contractions that leave us in pain.
   - Breathing deeply into and through painful moments is a very real and instant way of calming the nervous system.
   - Breathe and focus on the sensations of breath at any moment in order to reestablish being centered and grounded.
   - This is effective for physical, mental, emotional, and spiritual pain.
   - The more often your teen makes contact with their breath, the more effective it will become in grounding and centering.

9. **Sustain practices that promote health, especially including setting boundaries and eliminating toxic situations, people, chemicals, foods, and beverages.**
   - Invite your teen to make a commitment, and set daily intentions, to live healthfully in every way.

10. **Embrace inner wisdom and intuition as a guide and counterpoint to negative cognitions and beliefs.**
    - Offer permission to your teen, and invite her or him to tune inward and see if he or she can hear/feel/see/know the wise part of them that holds the wisdom of the universe.

    - The wisdom traditions suggest that we hold the truths of the universe before we are born, and then lose it all upon birth. The suggested purpose of being here on Earth is to learn it all again. The younger we are, the closer we are to the totality of the truths of the universe. As we get older, and have traumatic learning experiences, coupled with heavy emphasis on the provable, intuition and inner wisdom dim. For traumatized teens, it is crucial to recovery that they find and nurture any form of inner wisdom, that they can begin to trust and nurture. This process cultivates deep healing through self-empathy and highly effective self-compassion.

    - Finding and growing intuition and inner wisdom are very powerful antidotes to the harmful practices of abuse and trauma. Being hurt leaves memories and internalized negative beliefs that further damage the future of the traumatized individual. To counterbalance these negative effects, inner wisdom becomes a trusted friend who is always there.

    - It takes a long time to nurture intuition and inner wisdom. It is well worth the investment of time and sustained practice to do so whether you are a teen, parent, educator, and/or clinician.

11. **Graciously identify and receive gifts**
    - Traumatized teens can slip easily into depression. To counteract this propensity, a self-compassionate practice includes finding all the gifts that come your teen's way.

    - A gift can be a cancelled class, a great parking spot, or time with a good friend. It need not be a material item.

    - The more your teen notices "gifts," the more "gifts" will appear. It's the law of attraction coupled with the perceptual tendencies to find what we seek.

    - An example of this perceptual tendency is when you start to think of buying a certain kind of car, it suddenly appears more frequently on the road. It is more likely that your attention shifted to that kind of car, rather than a sudden explosion of sales in the car you're coincidentally interested in.

    - Graciously receiving gifts is also important to increasing the flow of gifts. This includes being grateful, not only with the words *thank you*, but also deep within the heart.

12. **Actively reduce stress and increase joyful activities**
    - Help your teen avoid activities and people that cause stress.

    - Facilitate the discovery of and involvement in things that bring joy.

- It is self-compassionate to act to relive suffering. One way of doing so is by reducing stress, and increasing pleasure.

- Healing happens when people can rest, play, find joy, and begin to live in alignment with their true nature.

13. **Ask for and receive help when needed**

- Like identifying and graciously receiving gifts, asking for and receiving help is just as important and challenging for traumatized teens.

- Having been traumatized can create trust issues, which prevent teens from asking for and accepting help.

- Please remind your teen that asking for and taking assistance when needed is an act of self-compassion and one to be taken as often as needed in order to heal.

- Help them see that some people will be trustworthy and helpful, while others may not. As they try to ask for help, they will learn more about whom they can and cannot trust. This cycle of trying and failing, learning, and trying again repeats itself throughout the lifespan.

14. **Welcome trustworthy people into your life**

- This is as easy as setting a daily intention to welcome trustworthy people.

- It's another example of the law of attraction, along with the perceptual tendency to find that which we seek.

- The more teens set their attention on welcoming trustworthy people in their life, the more trustworthy people will show up.

15. **Practice loving kindness for your mind, body, emotions, soul, other people, the environment, animals, and all beings everywhere**

- The loving kindness practice described in Chapter 1, Practice 4, is crucial for healing traumatized teens.

- Metta is a direct route to retraining attention and brain connections so that kindness is the predominant way of being.

- Encourage teens to extend their loving kindness practice to their mind, body, soul, other people (as is typical in the practice) as well as animals, and all beings everywhere.

- This kind of practice softens one's approach to life, which also promotes healing from trauma.

- It also creates a loving kindness mindset, which lends warmth and tenderness to every interaction and action.

16. **Invite and create opportunities for fun**

- Our true nature is to be in a state of joy, and yet we aren't able to have it 100% of the time.

- The juxtaposition of joy and pain creates the capacity for pleasure.

- Fun times and activities are a great way to return to that natural state of being after trauma.

- It is not easy to pursue fun when traumatized, however, this point in the protocol is meant to remind and emphasize the importance of fun in healing and recovering from trauma.

- Any kind of play and enjoyment is encouraged and recommended with the same priority and importance as medication or any other intervention.

17. **Positive reality: Focus on what you want**

- This is a reminder to your teen to let go of any thoughts, ideas, and beliefs that do not serve the highest good.

- This goes beyond kind self-talk to the release of any and all stories that are not in alignment with your teen's highest good.

- Help teens use language that speaks in the positive frame about what they truly want, whatever it is that their heart longs for; let that be the focus of their communication.

- This is a gentle way of redirecting negative self-talk or beliefs to a more self-compassionate place.

18. **Honor your unique needs and talents**

- Although we know we are all unique, there are so many ways we are clumped together and expected to behave the same.

- A self-compassionate approach to the unique needs of traumatized teens involves gently reminding them to honor their uniqueness.

- This is more important in the recovery from trauma because uniqueness can be internalized as damaged, disgusting, unlovable, and worse.

- Dr. Seuss said it best:

> Today you are YOU,
> that is truer than true.
> There is NO ONE alive
> That is YOUER than
> YOU!

- Tell your traumatized teen what Dr. Seuss said. It is permission to be who they are right now, which is one of the most potent healing elements of authentic empathy, and also the birthplace of compassion and self-compassion.

- Do not assume your teen knows this. Tell them often.

19. **Have open and honest communication with respect for all life**
    - Encourage your teen to speak openly and honestly with those they trust.
    - Invite them to be as honest as they can with themselves.
    - It takes courage and bravery to open to the truth in any moment.
    - Remind your traumatized teen how very strong they truly are.

20. **Allow things to be in their own time, starting with yourself**
    - Healing trauma takes a long time.
    - Healing takes patience.
    - It takes effort and a lot of energy.
    - The more time and energy applied to healing, the more effective it is.
    - Each one of us is endowed with self-healing properties; our bodies know exactly how to heal cuts and wounds. We also have everything within us to heal mental, emotional, and spiritual wounds.
    - Facilitate your teen having all the space he or she needs to feel safe and to heal wounds.

Reflect

- The components of this protocol may not be comfortable for all teens. They are invited to use the ones that feel right, modify those that can be, and discard those that do not resonate.

- For this unique population, it is important to start here, and perhaps restrict all self-compassion training to the protocol. The protocol is sufficient for initiating a self-compassion practice, and need not be expanded on until such time as your teen decides so.

2. SELF-COMPASSION FOR SHAME

Learn

Being victimized is associated with intense shame, which leads to secrecy, silence, and judgment (Brown, 2012). The more traumatized teens hide the shameful parts of their abuse or victimization, the more the shame grows and thrives. According to Brown, releasing shame comes from having the courage to be vulnerable, show the shame that exists, bring it into the light, and begin along a path of self-acceptance. The degree to which you practice authentic and consistent self-acceptance will determine the degree to which you can truly help your teen do the same.

Practice

This practice is a reminder to cultivate:

- Self-acceptance

- Nonjudgment (toward self and others)

- Self-kindness

Reflect

- Cultivating self-acceptance, nonjudgment, and self-kindness can be very challenging for teens who have been treated badly and subsequently internalized negative beliefs about themselves.

- Gentle and playful self-reminders to suspend judgment, reverse unkind thoughts or beliefs, and to consider self-acceptance are helpful. Setting daily intentions declares what your teen wants to gain, create, and/or develop. Doing so increases the likelihood that they will reach their goals.

3. STOP AND SOOTHE

Learn

Watkins and Watkins's Ego-States Therapy is based on the concept that a person's mind is comprised of different ego states—a collection of internal selves representing different ages and/or roles. This is not the same as dissociative identity disorder, however, it is a prominent feature of traumatized individuals. For traumatized teens training in self-compassion, the following practice can help re-regulate in moments of distress by tuning into and calming the fragmented ego part. It requires the assistance of a therapist to effectively impart to a traumatized teen.

Practice

Use the worksheet that follows to help your teen identify ages and or roles they played that are associated with trauma.

- Completing this worksheet increases your teen's mindful awareness of the events, ages, and roles that hold negative memories and beliefs.

- When your teen becomes distressed, one way for them to return to a calm state in the present moment is by tuning into the younger part or role that needs immediate attention. When the event occurred, the part of self that experienced it may have become dissociated and dislodged from the personality structure in order to survive the trauma. As such, your teen and their younger part *both* need comfort to move forward and onward.

- If possible, your teen can tune into that younger part and offer kind words such as:

"It's okay, it's all over now. We are all safe."

(Or anything that is comforting to them in the moment.)

Reflect

- This practice engages the inner nurturing object to soothe and heal neglected, wounded, and fragmented ego parts.

- It takes preparation in therapy sessions for teens to be able to use this in a moment of disturbance.

STOP AND SOOTHE

Age	Role (i.e., son/daughter/friend/student)	Event	Negative belief	Positive belief

FINDING SAFE AND TRUSTWORTHY PEOPLE

Learn

How do teens create safe and trusting relationships when they have been hurt? Maltreatment leads to alienation because the threat of further harm and abuse are expected. Additionally, the "trance of unworthiness" described by clincial psychologist, author, and meditation teacher Tara Brach, overwhelms traumatized teens with the sense that they don't deserve to be happy, which results in increased isolation. These negative effects on interpersonal connection must be overcome gently and patiently for self-compassion to arise. The element of common humanity in self-compassion is particularly hard for traumatized teens to cultivate because trust is an intervening variable. Help traumatized teens learn how to differentiate between safe people and unsafe people to build their ability to trust. Help your teen learn about this with the worksheet that follows.

Practice

Fill out the worksheet on the next page.

Reflect

- Invite your teen to fill in the worksheet with you. Offer your help to discuss the various people in your teen's life, and how safe or unsafe they may be.

- Be sure to use critical thinking and explore people in positions of authority who may or may not be trustworthy. The safety teachings in early years encourage children to seek the help of police officers, for example, however, this could be deadly, especially for male teens for color. As such, invite your teen to look critically at those they may take for granted as "safe."

- Look at the ways your teen feels entitled to goodness and having good people in his or her life. Just opening dialogue about this sends your teen's development in the direction of self-compassion.

THE PEOPLE IN MY LIFE

Safe people (name names)	Qualities of safe people	Unsafe people (name names)	Qualities of unsafe people	Tips for finding cool people

5. SELF-COMPASSION DECREASES PTSD SYMPTOMS AND NEGATIVE BEHAVIORS

Learn

Self-compassion is associated with a decrease in symptoms of PTSD and the negative behaviors that may occur (Neff, 2011). For example, cutting and using substances to cope with the negative effects of trauma are inconsistent with self-compassion practices. The precept of self-kindness implores traumatized teens to find gentler, kinder, more heart-centered ways of coping with their pain. This choice arises from intrinsic motivation and courage to face difficulties head on, resulting from the practice of self-compassion.

Practice

- When traumatized teens are faced with coping challenges, flashbacks, and triggers, they need a safe harbor to retreat to.

- Any self-compassion practice is a safe harbor.

- Help your teen see the value of self-compassion practice in coping with PTSD.

- Encourage your teen to value the strength, the community, and the gentle healing that comes with sustained commitment to practice self-compassion.

Reflect

- If self-compassion practice is not appealing to your traumatized teen, don't push it.

- Accepting your traumatized teen exactly as they are is the most compassionate way you can treat them. Doing so sets the tone so they can also treat themselves with compassion. This practice is only a gentle reminder to talk about the benefits of self-compassion with traumatized teens.

6. CURIOSITY AS A FORM OF SELF-KINDNESS

Learn

Self-kindness is a way of honoring vulnerabilities, pain, hurt, sensitivities, and uniqueness. One way to begin doing so is by getting curious about one's internal workings. Take time to turn inward. Exploring emotions, thoughts, memories, and experiences are ways of becoming more self-compassionate through increased intrapersonal mindful awareness.

Practice

Use the following script with your teen.

- Take a deep breath all the way down into your belly.

- Feel anchored in your seat, with feet firmly planted on the floor.

- Just notice whatever comes up.

- It may be disturbing or pleasurable; just notice.

- See how many things you can learn about yourself by paying attention to yourself.

List them all here:

1. _____

2. _____

3. _____

4. _____

5. _____

6. _____

Ask you teen to share anything they learned about themselves while paying attention for that moment.

Modification

Hand your teen a piece of paper. After encouraging her or him to take 3 deep breaths in to the belly, invite her or him to write anything that comes to mind, particularly about themselves.

Reflect

- Becoming curious about oneself can be very frightening; What was it like for you to tune inward, and observe your internal process?

- Do you lean towards your internal world with curiosity, or lean away?

7. "BE THE CHANGE YOU WISH TO SEE IN THE WORLD." — GHANDI

Learn

Be the change you wish to see in the world by focusing on the goodness within. Nurture it and watch it blossom. The more you become the person you respect, the more you will attract what you want and expect. Moreover, respecting your desires, and mirroring what you admire in the world as you wish it would be cultivates more of the same.

Practice

- Write down all your positive qualities. Don't hold back, let loose and record them all!

- Circle the top three that most stand out to you.

Reflect

- How might you intentionally position yourself to experience yourself in the best way possible?

- How might you create opportunities to join programs that allow you to experience these qualities?

(8.) THE ROLE OF TEARS

Learn

Crying is not only for sadness but associated with a range of emotions from joy to empathy to relief, grief, anger, and even surprise. It is also associated with physical cleansing of the eye—it removes debris that enters by flooding the eye and moving it out. On an emotional and spiritual level, crying does the very same, it cleanses. Sometimes it feels cathartic to cry, other times it is plain exhausting. The act of crying relieves the nervous system of pressure and pain that build up. Invite your teen to interpret crying in this way. For males, it may counter the prevailing gender stereotype of vulnerability and weakness associated with crying. For females, it reinforces strength in facing pain and the willingness to release it. This positive reframe is imperative to releasing the negative effects of trauma.

Another benefit of crying is that it elicits "social bonding and human connection." (Oaklander, 2016). It is one way of indicating to yourself, and to others, that there is a concern that is, for the moment, unbearable. In her 2016 article, Oaklander wrote that "noncrying people had a tendency to withdraw and described their relationships as less connected. They also experienced more negative aggressive feelings, like rage, anger and disgust, than people who cried." Crying has the power to connect people, which is well known to produce oxytocin and a sense of well-being. For these reasons, a good cry with another person may be even more beneficial than just crying alone. It is also helpful because it signals vulnerability and need. While this doesn't feel good to the person crying, it tells others they need help. It alerts people in their mirror neuron system to engage others with kind, empathic, and compassionate action. Traumatized teens need this kind of help, and tears are biologically coded to communicate this so oxytocin can be produced and healing can continue.

Practice

- Cry.

- Whenever your teen feels the need to cry, allow it.

- Encourage your teen to honor themselves, their losses, hurts, pains, and traumas by crying when the need arises.

- This is not a sign of weakness; rather it is a strength to face pain straight on and be willing to let it go.

- Cry with a trusted friend, therapist, or even a parent if it feels right and comfortable.

Reflect

- Ever have a good cry?

- Explore any negative associations your teen may have with crying. Take time to truly understand this. Ask questions and understand why crying may not be something your teen wants to do.

9. TEND AND BEFRIEND

Learn

Tend and befriend is an innate response to stress where people care for young or vulnerable people (tend) and reach out to others for support and community (befriend) (Germer, 2009). This response is linked to oxytocin, a hormone connected to feelings of social safeness, well-being, and a sense of being loved and wanted (Gilbert, 2009). The soothing system that produces oxytocin is essential to well-being, and an important component of self-compassion. Volunteer efforts are an act of generosity that appears to be as pleasurable, if not more so, than receiving help. When people witness others giving charity, the same pleasure centers in the brain come alive as when they receive money themselves. Tending to others increases oxytocin, and results in feelings of social connection and well-being. A study found participants who spent money on others were much happier than those who spent money on themselves (Dunn et al., 2008).

Practice

Research demonstrates that giving to others benefits the giver more than the receiver, and causes oxytocin to flow.

- Create opportunities to volunteer with your traumatized teen.

- Encourage traumatized teens to give to others in small ways.

- The flow of effort outward to benefit others will serve a healing function for your teen.

- Promote giving in amounts that feel right to your teen. This is not a "more is better" kind of thing. Any giving is good. Too much can be maladaptive and have the reverse effect.

Reflect

- Explore your relationship to giving and see if you can increase your practice with your teen.

- Discuss the difference between giving time and money to help others.

- Identify people your teen may want to connect with and offer compassion.

9 Self-Compassion Training for LGBTQ Teens

According to the Centers for Disease Control, almost a third of LGBTQ teens have suffered violence or sexual assault. Bullying, lack of acceptance by families, epidemic rates of homelessness and sex work, as well as being shamed and rejected by adults in their lives contribute to increased amounts of suffering. The suffering increases exponentially when the LGBTQ teen is also a person of color, and/or poor. The intersection of these variables contributes to this population being at highest risk for suicide and, therefore, in greatest need for self-compassion training, as one means of increasing resilience, healing, and survival.

DISCLAIMER: Due to the high level of trauma sustained by LGBTQ youth, the Self-Compassion Training Protocol for Traumatized Teens must be used with this population, in addition to those practices specifically formulated for LGBTQ youth.

(1.) GENDER FLUIDITY

Learn

None of us is *either* man *or* woman. Truly, we are all made up of elements of both and express one or the other, or both, to varying degrees. Though commonly used interchangeably, *gender* and *sex* are not the same. Gender refers to the identity, interests, and expressions that differentiate between the sexes, while sex refers to the chromosomes, gonads, sex hormones, and internal reproductive organs a person is born with. Gender expression is the outward presentation of one's gender role, wired in the brain and not in the genes or genitals. Gender identity is tied to an internal sense of being female, male, both, or neither. The diversity of human gender presentation causes a great deal of problems for gender nonconforming youth, who are forced into binaries that fit genitals but not necessarily with their neuronal wiring and genetic makeup.

Gender theorists argue vehemently for gender expansiveness, where gender is neither tied to genitals nor a fixed binary. A gender binary means people are either female or male, however, this is not an accurate label for people who are genderqueer or gender nonconforming, and for the rest of the population enjoying their gender identity as an amalgam of both or neither. Carl Jung described each one of us as being comprised of *amina* and *animus*, with *anima* being stronger in woman, and *animus* dominant in men. *Anima* is the feminine archetype, while *animus* is the masculine. This archetype may be represented by the yin and yang symbol, which calls forth the universality of this concept. To further support the universality of human nongender, in some societies it is appropriate for men to hold hands and wear skirts, while this may be unusual in most North American cities.

The following two practices are appropriate for all teens, regardless of whether or not they personally identify as LGBTQ. It will increase their mindful awareness, self-empathy, self-kindness, and common humanity—all of which contribute to self-compassion.

Practice I

- Three millennials who are challenging gender norms are: EJ Johnson, Jaden Smith, and Ruby Rose. By boldly eschewing gender norms mixed with their celebrity, they are introducing this generation to fluid forms of gender expression that are not circumscribed by genitals and social convention. Their gift to humanity lies in embracing the universal experience of both genders in varying degrees.

- Invite your teen to look at photos of Jaden Smith, EJ Johnson, and Ruby Rose.

- Collect the photos, and analyze them according to:

    - Norms broken.

    - The ways they appeal/don't appeal to you.

Practice II

> **TRANSWOMAN:** an individual who was assigned as male at birth and identifies as a woman.
>
> **GENDERQUEER:** any individual who identified outside of the gender binary
>
> **AGENDER:** an individual who identified as having no gender
>
> **TWO SPIRIT:** an aboriginal person who identifies with or fulfills multiple gender roles traditionally found in aboriginal culture
>
> **TRANSMAN:** an individual who was assigned female at birth and identifies as a man.

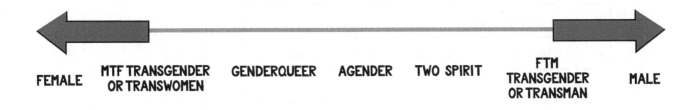

FEMALE   MTF TRANSGENDER   GENDERQUEER   AGENDER   TWO SPIRIT   FTM TRANSGENDER   MALE
          OR TRANSWOMEN   OR TRANSMAN

- Place a line on the spectrum to indicate where your gender identity lies.

- There is no right or wrong answer, and you can come back and change it whenever you like.

- The placement of the line on the spectrum will depend on how much or how little you embrace one or both genders.

- Think about how much feminine or masculine stuff you like. It's not necessary to think of what society thinks you should like, but rather what your heart says is the most important thing here.

Reflect

- Assist your teen in determining where their gender lies.

- Explore what it means to your teen for gender to be fluid.

2. SEXUAL FLUIDITY

Learn

Like gender, sexuality is also fluid. Some people are more attracted to people of the same sex and/or gender, others are more attracted to those of the opposite sex and/or gender, while many more are attracted to both in varying degrees and at different times. Kinsey created a scale to represent the diversity of sexuality, and the one below offers 2 additional categories to reflect modern times:

Practice

1	Heterosexual
2	Mostly heterosexual, sometimes homosexual
3	Bisexual
4	Mostly homosexual, sometimes heterosexual
5	Homosexual
6	Pansexual - a person of any gender who is sexually attracted to people of all genders
7	Aromantic - interested in sex without romance
8	Asexual

- Place a line on the spectrum to indicate where your sexual attraction lies.

- There is no right or wrong answer and you can come back and change it whenever you like.

- The placement of the line on the spectrum will depend on how much or how little you are attracted to the opposite, same, or both genders.

- If you don't have any sexual attraction, that is also okay. Accept it with loving allowance.

- Think about how interested you are in sex stuff with people of the same, opposite, and/or both genders. This isn't an inventory about whom you actually have sexual relations with, but rather who you are interested in.

- It's unnecessary to think of what society thinks you should like, but rather what your heart says is most important here.

Reflect

- Explore the level of self and social acceptance around your teen concerning issues of sexuality.

3. COMING OUT TO FREEDOM: SOCIAL MENTALITY THEORY

Learn

Paul Gilbert (2009) calls social mentalities "the way our minds seek out other minds to have different types of interaction with" (p. 100). When LGBTQ teens want to find connection and common humanity, despite feeling different from the dominant culture, social mentalities guide them in how to meet their needs. A social mentality shapes actions, beliefs, and values, and helps you determine when the relationship you seek is found. Social mentality produces the inner experiences, such as thoughts and feelings, that maintain relationships. With a social mentality, the rise of positive feelings is associated with the relationship working, and negative feelings with it not working well (Gilbert, 2009).

For LGBTQ teens, social mentality guides them away from dominant expectations, standards, and conventions. It can cause conflict with some, while promoting connection with others. Statistics suggest that 20–40% of homeless youth are LGBTQ, despite only making up about 10% of the population. For many LGBTQ teens, coming out can lead to family rejection. For this reason, helping LGBTQ teens come out when and how they are ready, while also promoting the development of healthy social mentalities, can literally save lives. LGBTQ teens incidentally also have disproportional suicide rates.

Practice

- LGBTQ teens are encouraged to access all the support needed to come out and cultivate healthy social mentalities.

- Find others/peers/adults/communities/social groups that support and facilitate the development of healthy LGBT identity.

- Finding common humanity in coming out has two elements:

  a. Discovering a happy and healthy community of peers and supportive elders.

  b. Remembering that you are among many others before you, and after you, who have/may suffer rejection for being LGBTQ.

- Respect that the social mentality for LGBTQ youth is different from that of other teens, and create space and time to learn how.

Reflect

- Take private time to reflect on prejudices, judgments, and biases you hold toward being LGBTQ. Invite your teen to discuss any he or she may have.

- Explore the resources and supports available in your community to help your teen come out and find a community that feels right.

(4.) COLLECTIVE TRAUMATIZATION

Learn

Larry Yang speaks of the assumptions and conventions about sexuality and gender that collectively traumatize LGBTQ individuals. *Collective trauma* is the widespread psychological effect shared by a group of people of any size who witnesses or experiences trauma. Trauma can be seen as too much, too soon. Social rejection is something everyone experiences at some point. Some rejections build tenacity and persistence, while others contribute to devastation. For the LGBTQ community, there is traumatic impact on the entire community resulting from embracing authentic nature that runs in opposition to the dominant cultural expectations. While this cultural trend is opening to greater inclusivity, youngsters are expected to grow up straight, and declare their sexuality only when it differs from the cultural norm.

Practice

- Find a community where common humanity is the theme, and LGBTQ individuals are welcome and included fully.

- The search for common humanity is one way for LGBTQ teens to heal the collective trauma they are exposed to.

- Let the community be open-minded to people and ideas from all racial and ethnic groups with emphasis on inclusiveness.

- Look for groups of people who listen deeply to lesbian, gay, bisexual, and transsexual teens and help to increase awareness of their needs.

- Economic inclusion, financial support, and scholarship shall be prioritized in organizations LGBTQ teens consider joining.

Reflect

- Discuss the examples of collective trauma your LGBTQ teen has heard of, seen, or experienced.

- Brainstorm together about places where your teen can join in for safety and common humanity around being LGBTQ.

- By bringing up this topic, your teen learns that you are an authentic ally.

(5.) SHAME AND LGBTQ TEENS

Learn

Shame is deeply connected to themes learned from social conventions, the culture, parental teachings, and educational policy. The way we see, think about, and treat ourselves is connected to the way others have treated us. From parents, to siblings, teachers, friends, and more, teens have a lot of opinions to filter as their identity comes together. These opinions can be unintentionally shaming for LGBTQ teens, and the shame of being rejected and different can move into the realm of trauma. For this reason, the **Self-Compassion Training Protocol for Traumatized Teens** is highly recommended for use in tandem with the foregoing practices.

Practice

- Explore memories and experiences that have been traumatizing and shame inducing for your teen.

- Being LGBTQ is a beautiful expression of the diversity of human love and existence.

- Invite your teen to find self-kindness around themselves, their identity, and the harsh ways others have reacted to them.

Reflect

- This practice is geared toward a dialogue about shame. Just having this dialogue with your LGBTQ teen promotes their practice of self-compassion.

- Be brave and open the dialogue, even if it is uncomfortable.

- The act of opening this dialogue gives air to shame, which eliminates the secrecy, silence, and judgment upon which it thrives (Brown, 2012).

6. "IT'S ALL DRAG, REALLY." (JAY MICHAELSON, 2014)

Learn

The late Rita Gross was a Buddhist scholar, practitioner, and teacher who explored gender identity from diverse religious perspectives. She taught that being male or female is not fixed; realizing this leads to fluidity and freedom of expression that respects the inherent impermanence in everything and everyone. Appreciating this nonfixed, fluid state of gender and sexuality increases enlightened self-understanding by removing limitations to being human.

Practice

Teach your teen about *annata*.

- *Annata* is the state of self that is ever changing.

- By realizing the self is always changing, you can open yourself to a host of identities. It's like being in drag at all times because the "true you" is truly changing at every moment.

- Being straight, lesbian, gay, bisexual, transgender, and/or queer and questioning are all different masks we can put on our ever changing core self.

- It may feel fixed and concrete. That's okay.

- Your relationship to yourself will change over time.

- Embrace the freedom of infinite possibility by knowing you can be anyone you choose to be, simply by saying so and living so.

- Those who cling to dominant stereotypes risk injuring the self that is happiest when free, expansive, and open to possibility.

Reflect

- Though inclusion and belonging are important aspects of adolescence, the art of self-acceptance in the face of constant change is the birthplace of self-compassion.

- By exploring *annata* with your LGBTQ teen, you empower them to think kindly about themselves when they feel different and/or ostracized.

7. PRONOUNS MATTER

Learn

For teens with gender identity fluidity already crystallizing, the choice of pronouns used to communicate with and about them, is critical. For those who are queer and/or questioning, the commonplace practice of using pronouns based on apparent gender can be an empathic failure and source of harm. The following practice, enlightens adult caregivers of teens about the various pronouns, so they can facilitate self-compassion for the teen in their lives.

Practice

- "Ze" and "Mx." are two pronouns used to by people who neither identify as male or female.

- "They" is another pronoun for queer teens. It refers to the singular person, rather than a group.

Reflect

- Discuss the pronouns with your teen.

- Ask them how they want to be referred to, and know this is a high level of empathy and respect to do so.

- Assuming the gender of another person can be traumatic to non-conforming teens. Taking the time to ask how they wish to be referred to not only represents empathy and kindness, but also promotes self-compassion because it tells teens they are free to be their true authentic self.

10 Self-Compassion Training for Teens with Substance Abuse Concerns

Teens struggling with substance abuse concerns can benefit from training in self-compassion practice. Starting with acceptance of suffering, and of the attempt to self-soothe with substances, this chapter presents practices and tools for initiating or maintaining recovery. Self-compassion begins with mindful awareness practices and incorporates self-kindness, common humanity, and the willingness to act to relieve suffering. Self-compassion also arises when teens acknowledge the grip of addiction that causes suffering.

1. RIDING THE WAVE OF CRAVE

Learn

The acceptance of suffering as a component of being human is one step forward toward recovery from substance abuse and addiction. When teens know suffering is likely to arise, and you should be prepared with healthy coping strategies, it is possible for them to prevail even in difficult moments. When teens can't cope with suffering, turning to substances to numb pain is a common maladaptive response. The following practice cultivates mindful awareness around suffering, cravings, and using substances. It is intended merely as one step toward mindful awareness in the art of cultivating self-compassion.

Practice

• When you feel an urge to use your substance of choice, please think about the event that happened one nanosecond before the craving came on.

• See if you can notice the emotions that come up as a result of the event.

• If you can, just try to notice the sensations in your body, with patience, and kindness.

• See if the craving will subside.

• Offer yourself compassion, by saying something like this to yourself:

**"This is what craving/suffering/feeling
[whichever is most appropriate for you] feels like in my body."**

"This is part of being human, and suffering sometimes."

**"May I be kind to myself in this moment, and
offer myself the compassion I need."**

• When ready, record this event in the worksheet that follows.

• Try to lovingly accept yourself even if you use a substance.

• This is a practice in self-acknowledgment and self-acceptance when suffering.

• You don't have to be perfect, you are already good enough beyond measure!

Reflect

• This self-report inventory prompts teens to begin paying attention to what causes them to suffer, how they feel when suffering is triggered, and whether or not they use a substance to cope.

• It is at once a training activity in mindful awareness, and also a reminder to teens to offer themselves compassion for suffering, for trying to relieve their suffering, and for the experience of being human.

SELF-REPORT INVENTORY

Date	Time	Trigger event	Feelings	Did you use? Yes/No	Did you offer yourself self-compassion for suffering?

(2.) <u>RELAPSE</u>

Learn

Relapse is a common element of recovery. It doesn't happen to everyone, however, when it does kindness and forgiveness are truly helpful in moving onward and forward with recovery. Prepare your teen for the possibility that relapse may occur. It softens the disappointment if/when it occurs, and promotes realignment with a path of recovery.

Practice

- If/when relapse occurs, say silently to yourself:

> **"It's okay, I am still a good person even though I messed up."**

Reflect

- For some people, relapse can be a slippery slope spiraling down toward worthlessness.

- Does making a mistake leave your teen feeling worthless? If so, this may be a barrier to recovery.

- Bring mindful awareness, kindness, forgiveness, and inspiration to move forward and onward when relapse and mistakes happen.

3. SANGHA FOR RECOVERY FROM SUBSTANCE ABUSE

Learn

Substance abuse and addiction are associated with difficulty coping, isolation, and strong neural linkages between substances and relief of suffering. *Sangha* is Pali for "community," and a main element of Buddhist practices. Psychology and research data acknowledge the value of Buddhist practices in healing suffering (Gilbert, 2009). Sangha is the sense of belonging that comes with joining a community of like-minded members. Twelve-step programs rely on the power of community in promoting recovery. Self-compassion reminds us of the common humanity that is suffering and trying to cope with suffering. By joining a community of other teens suffering with addiction and working toward recovery, self-compassion is present and promoting healing.

Noah Levine's *Refuge Recovery* (2014) offers a new look at suffering from substance abuse in terms of not only ending the suffering of addiction but also contributing to the healing of all human suffering through the interconnectedness of all life. Levine introduces us to a high level of shared humanity when he contextualizes recovery from addiction in the recovery of all humankind from any kind of suffering. When one person tends to his or her recovery, that person promotes health and well-being for his- or herself, and others too. This is the healing source of self-compassion because it respects shared humanity in the face of individual suffering and efforts related to easing pain.

Practice

Contemplate this statement:

> **When you commit to your own recovery, you
> promote health and wellness for all beings everywhere.**

Reflect

- In what ways is your teen's substance abuse/recovery linked to other people?

- Does your teen feel supported by a community?

④ THE FOUR PILLARS OF DRUG USE

Learn

According to Siegel (2013), there are four reasons why teens use substances:

1. **Experiment**

2. **Connect socially**

3. **Self-medicate**

4. **Addiction**

These four reasons are tied to other basic needs that may not be getting met at the time.

Practice

• Using NVC (Chapter 4, Practice 4), help your teen identify the unmet needs that promote experimenting with mind- altering substances, taking risks to connect with a peer group, self-medicating pain, and/or addiction and dependency.

• Find alternative ways for your teen to get these needs met.

Reflect

• Is your teen seeking to expand their mind and experience wider states of consciousness? If so, promote meditation, mindful awareness practices, and time alone in nature.

• Is your teen using substances because their friends are? Prioritize your teen's safety and promote limits and boundaries around friends who use and provide substances. Face the conflict and pain of limit setting, and trust your teen needs limits more than friends who use drugs.

• Is your teen using substances because they are in pain, and need to anesthetize themselves? If so, seek the support of licensed mental health clinicians to determine the best course of treatment.

• Is your teen using substances because any of the first three reasons for using drugs have led to tolerance, dependency, and addiction? The cycle of use can be explained by the hypersensitization that occurs when people become addicted to substances. Repeated use of a substance produces hypersensitization—a greater neurobehavioral response to future uses of the same substance. The addicted brain develops incentive salience to the drug of choice, which takes liking it to the next level. Incentive salience keeps the cycle fueled and operating at full capacity. These associations are strong, and last well after sobriety is established. As a result, addiction requires specialized support. Please seek intensive daily outpatient or inpatient treatment if your teen has an addiction.

11 Self-Compassion Training for Teens with Autism

Teens with autism represent another unique population for training in self-compassion, especially those with severe communication difficulties. Self-compassion training for teens with autism emphasizes self-soothing, self-regulation, and naming of emotions to reduce outbursts and emotional contagion. Just like social skills training explicitly teaches youngsters with autism about relating to others, self-compassion training takes a similar approach in simplifying the concepts of mindfulness, shared humanity, and kindness to oneself in terms teens with autism can relate to. Special attention is offered to how teens with autism cultivate self-compassion in relation to their play, complex stereotypical mannerisms (stimming), sexual development, their response to treatment protocols, as well as their fit in a culture that rejects their natural way of being.

DISCLAIMER: Self-compassion practice is a self-initiated practice. For teens with autism, it is unlikely they will want to initiate a practice. The activities offered here are intended to help adult caregivers shift their thinking about autism to be more compassionate. In so doing, interventions, lesson planning, and life structure will have compassion at the heart and indirectly promote self-compassion in teens with autism.

1. HOW TO TALK ABOUT SELF-COMPASSION WITH TEENS WHO HAVE AUTISM

Learn

Though teens with autism are chronologically and physically approaching adulthood, their development is delayed in various areas. Discussing self-compassion with teens who have cognitive deficits and impairments can be challenging. The goal is to simplify the concepts and verbalize the actions and steps while doing it with your teen. Here are some basic ways to introduce self-compassion.

Practice

- Ask your teen if they remember a time when someone was nice to them.

- Help them find the words to describe what the other person did that was nice. Use reflective listening and add new words to help your teen with autism learn what it means to be kind.

- If the person is a friend, ask if your teen would like them to be her or his own best friend.

- Discuss the joys of being nice/kind to yourself.

- Ask your teen if they were ever suffering in some way and someone helped them. What was it like?

- Use reflective listening so your teen can truly hear what it was like for them to receive kindness in a moment of suffering (i.e., repeat your teen's statement in your own words, avoid adding information, opinions, or interpretations.)

- Discuss the possibility of your teen being their own good friend who is kind and helpful when they are struggling.

- Tell your teen that everyone struggles and suffers in some way, at some time. Help your teen remember this whenever times get tough. It may not be meaningful to teens with autism to know they are part of a community of people who suffer, but it is one way to begin imparting self-compassion.

Reflect

- Teens with autism don't need to be introduced to self-compassion to learn some practices. They need exposure and explicit direction. This practice introduces it to them in a subtle way.

- This is a one-off practice you can do with your teen with autism. It is not intended for sustained practice by teens.

2. SELF-SOOTHING AND SELF-REGULATING FOR TEENS WITH AUTISM

Learn

Some experts believe people with autism aren't suffering from an empathy deficit but rather overempathize, which results in dysregulation and subsequent avoidance. Some believe those with autism are fully capable of empathy and compassion once they are alerted to the social cues, and learn how to read them. Since people with autism are able to form attachments to one or two individuals, and/or pets, the logic doesn't hold that they completely lack empathic capacity. As such, the question of who is suffering and lacking empathy becomes an issue. It's as if neurotypical people can't cope with the difference in relating presented by people with autism. A lack of empathy for their unique propensity drives Applied Behavior Analysis and behavior modification approaches. This other angle of looking at teens with autism would result in a high degree of mindful awareness of what it means to have autism and subsequent difficulty relating with others. It offers teens with autism an opportunity to be kind to themselves when they see others being kind to them and teaching them self-acceptance.

Practice

- Teach your teen about autism and empathy.

- Help your teen learn that it feels bad sometimes when we connect with others, and that it is normal to avoid things that don't feel good.

- Invite your teen with autism to practice tuning into others, and then adjusting themselves to the information they receive when they tune in. Just paying attention to another person may be flooding for teens with autism, which is why self-soothing and self-regulation practices are important.

- For teens with autism, self-regulation practices may look very different.

- They may include swinging, fast movements, pacing, and stimming.

- Offer autistic teens time and space for whatever they need to become regulated again.

Reflect

- It may seem counterintuitive to have a self-compassion practice focus on others.

- This one is intended to shore up teens with autism so they can encounter others more easily and frequently. It is a combination of scaffolding and exposure.

- When teens with autism can encounter others with empathy, they gain strength in tapping into common humanity. It is a very challenging and lengthy process, however, small steps like this initiate the process.

③ NAMING EMOTIONS

Learn

Naming emotions is a basic mindful awareness practice, and essential for teens with autism who struggle with social communication.

Practice

- Get a feeling chart with faces representing different emotions, or look at emojis on a smartphone.

- Discuss the different faces and feelings on the chart and connect them to recent events in your teen's life.

- Teens with autism need help making connections between themselves and other people. By discussing recent events in your teen's life as a reference point for the faces on the chart, you help your teen gain the language needed for mindful awareness, self-kindness, and ultimately self-compassion.

Reflect

- Help your teen learn how important it is to have words for emotions.

- This may seem like a very basic activity for teens, however, those with autism develop unevenly and this part is rather challenging. It is a necessary component of mindful awareness, and also of responsible and compassionate communication.

- It is not necessary to connect this practice with self-compassion when doing it with your teen. Your teen does not need to know it is a foundational skill of self-compassion, rather they need the explicit training.

(4.) <u>PLAY</u>

Learn

Play is a time when people are free, learning, moving, wondering, creating, and inventing. Sometimes play happens in groups, and sometimes it is a solo activity. For those with autism, the group aspect of play is less common, and solo play tends to be atypical. A self-compassionate approach to play respects the diverse ways people play and offers teens with autism permission to play however they like. While this may seem counterintuitive once again, to allow those with autism to do what they want when it is socially unacceptable it is actually one message of acceptance in a world that rejects them in most ways.

Practice

- If your teen has the cognitive ability to understand that some types of play are appropriate when alone, and not appropriate when around others, then introduce this practice.

- If your teen cannot discriminate between alone time and time with others, do not use this practice at all.

- Allow your teen specified time to play as he or she wishes. Offer no judgment about it, just accept it and allow it for the time agreed on.

- If transitions and stopping activities are particularly hard for your teen, you may wish to avoid this practice, or use it as a reward.

Reflect

- Teens with autism have many different levels of functioning.

- Accepting your teen's preferred kind of play initiates your teen's self-acceptance.

- This practice is a way of opening to innate tendencies with loving allowance, and simultaneously guiding them to the appropriate time and place.

5. SELF-COMPASSION FOR COMPLEX STEREOTYPICAL MANNERISMS (STIMMING)

Learn

Complex stereotypic mannerisms, also known as stimming, are a natural drive that when satisfied results in pleasure. To pathologize and deny teens opportunities for natural expression and resulting joy is an empathic failure to their inherent way of being. Barry Neil Kauffman is one parent who took empathy all the way when his son Ruan was diagnosed with autism. Kauffman mirrored his son completely until he gained his trust, and Ruan signaled some willingness for social engagement. Only then did he engage his son. At other times, he gave his son space to be. Ruan is now the director of Global Education for the Autism Treatment Center of America. This approach to treating autism was studied at Northwestern University and found to be effective, though there are criticisms to the program and it's delivery, which impact study findings. For our purposes, this story demonstrates how empathy and compassion for the unique needs of teens with autism looks very different from the programs, treatments, and diagnoses we commonly apply. By changing the way we see teens with autism and their unusual behaviors, we can help them become self-compassionate.

Practice

• Dedicate a time and place when and where your teen can be free to stim.

• Help them be free of judgment by empathizing with their needs, rather than the discomfort others feel around them.

• Minimize commentary from unempathic adults who come into your teen's life.

• If teens are nonverbal, mirroring their stimming is one way to provide empathy.

• Mirroring empathy heals and causes oxytocin to flow, which results in the experience of kindness and well-being. It lays the neuronal groundwork for your teen with autism to access later.

Reflect

• Explore your feelings about seeing your teen stim. Is it something that causes shame? Do you want it to stop because it agitates you? These are barriers to empathy for teens with autism—reducing them promotes compassion and self-compassion.

• What would you feel like if you were stimming like your teen with autism? Is it something you would avoid at all cost? Is there any way you could see yourself doing it for discrete periods of time?

• It is important to remove barriers to empathy for your teen with autism as it helps your teen cultivate self-empathy, the foundation of empathy, compassion, and self-compassion.

6. SELF-COMPASSION FOR PUBESCENT TEENS WITH AUTISM

Learn

Teens with autism go through puberty. Their bodies change and for some, sexual desire springs forth. This is a challenging time for neurotypical teens; for those with autism it gets even more complicated. Sexual development in teens with autism can involve others (willingly and/or unwillingly) and/or cause discomfort to others. In the case of teens gratifying themselves in public, there are real dangers of interaction with criminal justice, and subsequent maltreatment when the diagnosis is known, and also when it is not known. The practice that follows is a reminder to teach teens with autism about puberty, their changing bodies, and how, when, and where to gratify themselves. This is even more necessary for teens with autism because they have difficulty navigating social situations, let alone those that are sexually charged. Do not assume teens with autism do not have sexuality–they do. Do not assume teens with autism will not explore sex with others because they have social communication disorders—they may.

Teaching teens with autism about sex is related to self-compassion by informing them about how to behave with responsibility to themselves, and to others. Being able to create safety for oneself is an act of kindness that can prevent some suffering. It also recognizes that sexual development and desire are aspects common to humanity regardless of social communication challenges.

Practice

- Incorporate formal and explicit sexual education training into the programs of teens with autism.

- Explore the places, times, and people with whom sexual activity may take place. Be explicit. Include those where and with whom it is not allowed.

- Discuss the rule that prohibits sex with animals. It is important to say things that seem obvious to typical teens; it is not obvious to teens with autism and their ignorance could result in great suffering.

- Ask your teen to repeat the rules to make sure your teen received it as you intended.

Reflect

- What is it like to go into this level of detail about sexual development and desire with teens with autism?

- Do you have any discomfort with or barriers to this topic? Exploring your barriers is an act of self-compassion that promotes more of the same in your teen.

- Discuss these rules with your teen, and remind them that these rules are there for everyone's safety.

7. SELF-COMPASSION FOR TREATMENT PROTOCOLS

Learn

Applied Behavior Analysis and behavior modification programs aim to eliminate socially inappropriate behaviors, while increasing more desirable ones. Since those with autism do not conform to the social norms of our culture, the behaviors tend to be rather stubborn despite extensive therapies. Helping teens with autism cultivate a little self-compassion starts with accepting that the treatments may be very harsh and unwanted from their perspective. Giving them the words, and permission, to say when and if treatments are a problem for them creates opportunities for them to learn self-kindness. It's about opening a dialogue for empathy and self-empathy for your teen around treatments, not necessarily about making any changes unless so indicated.

Practice

- If your teen with autism is resisting therapies/treatments, give them room and words to express it all.

- Reflect it back, not only for empathy, but also so teens can have a second experience of self-empathy when they hear your words. The second experience of self-empathy will also serve as an act of self-compassion because being witnessed and seen again by themselves, and you, reduces suffering.

Reflect

- This practice is an invitation to explore the topic of treatment and therapies with increased empathy for your teen with autism. Doing so increases the voice of self-kindness that teens with autism can cultivate like echolalia.

⑧ SELF-COMPASSION FOR LIFE IN A CULTURE THAT REJECTS INNATE WAYS OF BEING

Learn

What if you were in a room with teens with autism, and they didn't know you were there while they were talking about life? One time when I had that opportunity, people with autism were complaining loudly about the harm done to them for playing in nonconforming ways. For them, it was tantamount to training lefties to write with their right hand, because it is the dominant way. Had I not heard it myself firsthand, I'm not sure I ever would have believed it. And having worked with children and adults with autism, this was a strangely uncharacteristic discussion. It made me rethink my empathy, and also how we treat people with autism. Promoting self-compassion in teens with autism invites us to reconsider whose problem it is that teens with autism are the way they are.

Practice

- Ask your teen what it's like to have autism.

- Listen for anything that suggests suffering from isolation, communication difficulties, stimming, or other sensory problems.

- Listen from your teen's perspective, and see what it is like.

Reflect

- When adults shift their perspective on caring for children, the experience changes for both.

- Compassion for teens with autism promotes the cultivation of self-compassion for both.

9. SELF-COMPASSION FOR SENSORY NEEDS

Learn

Autism is commonly associated with disorders of the vestibular system and with other senses as well. This may be why rocking, spinning, twirling, and swinging are typical complex stereotypic movements for people with autism. Ayers (2005) described the role of gravitational security on humans as being even more primal than the mother-child relationship. She suggested that gravitational security is the trust that we will always stand safely upon the earth. When a person's relationship to the ground beneath them is insecure, they may feel "lost in space" and other relationships may fail to thrive as a result of this insecure foundation. Vestibular disorders are also associated with digestion and learning problems.

Practice

• This practice simply involves appreciating the influence sensory integration has on your teen with autism, specifically if there are problems with the vestibular system.

• If your teen's cognitive ability is adequate, explain the role of gravity and the Earth's pull beneath their feet in creating security. Help them see the effects of this in their life, as well as the strategies they can use to mitigate them.

• "Fun is a child's word for sensory integration" (Ayres, 2005). When they are fully engaged and having fun, the sensory system is operating well. Create opportunities for fun, and tell your teen with autism why.

• Some examples of fun with sensory equipment include using scooter boards and receiving heavy pressure. This may work for some teens with autism, while others may be phobic to it. Work with an occupational therapist who is trained in sensory integration to find the right mix of strategies for your teen.

Reflect

• The limbic system is the part of the brain that decides which sensory input to attend to. Teens with autism have difficulty with this, and become overwhelmed with sensory input. Self-compassionate practices help them understand this.

• Think about how you feel when you are in an unfamiliar place, and you become disoriented and lost. How would you feel if you didn't recognize anything? Now, imagine this is what life can be like for your teen with autism, at times. With this in mind, how can you help her or him develop kindness for her- or himself in an environment that looks the same to you both, but *feels* very different to teens with autism.

• Help your teen with autism find words to understand why he or she doesn't like change, and how incredibly distressing it can be. Let your teen know there are many others similar to him or her, even if they aren't there in this moment.

(10.) GAMIFYING THE GROWTH MINDSET FOR TEENS WITH AUTISM

Learn

Self-kindness arises with mental flexibility, which is particularly challenging for those with autism. Growth mindset (Chapter 5, Practice 12) is the acceptance that we are all growing and changing, and with effort, skills and abilities can change. It is internally motivated and empirically validated (Dweck, 2006). When teens with autism play preferred games, and they hit a snag, it is an opportunity to cultivate self-kindness. Turn it into a game with them, and play away!

Practice

- Sit with your teen while they play a game of their choice, or play with your teen if possible.

- When your teen hits a block, offer words of encouragement that promote a growth mindset, like:

"With every miss, you learn what not to do next time."

"It's okay, keep playing and growing better and better at this game!"

Reflect

- For teens with autism, it is especially important to hear warm words of encouragement as a means of cultivating self-compassion. Their propensity towards echolalia, makes statements of self-kindness a learning opportunity for being self-compassionate.

(11.) "I DON'T WANT TO DO IT!" BRAIN

Learn

"Like the system that registers sensations, the 'I want to do it' system is working poorly in the child with autism" (Ayres, 2005). When presented with something new, teens with autism may resist. Teens benefit from compassion, and learn self-compassion, when helped to understand that the part of their brain that gets them going and doing stuff isn't working well.

Practice

Use these phrases to help your teen with autism motivate to do new and different things, even though her or his nervous system says NO!

"Even though I don't want to do this, I will."
"I am brave and try new things, even though they are scary."

Reflect

• Understanding the role of inhibited volition and activity initiation is an opportunity to help your teen with autism practice self-kindness and self-acceptance.

• Bringing words to the problem, and coaching your teen to use language that supports mixed feelings, offers empathy to heal the problem of the moment. The healing is itself an act of compassion, which leads to a cascade of self-compassion later on.

12 | Self-Compassion Training for Chronically and Terminally Ill Teens

Self-compassion practices for teens with chronic and terminal illnesses involve many of the same protocols and activities from previous chapters such as: Self-Compassion Training Protocol for Traumatized Teens, breath work for anxiety and depression, and practices connecting the mind and body. This chapter dives deeply into the concerns of death, dying, and profound and atypical suffering in adolescence. Existential questions, opportunities to examine meaning in life, purpose, and legacy are explored, and combined with self-reflective activities and gentle meditations for self-healing.

1. THE HEART TAP

Learn

This practice is designed to promote some instant relief of deep and profound suffering that includes high affective arousal, in the moment. This practice is not based in any healing or treatment modalities but rather serves as a rapid anchor for moments of extreme suffering.

Practice

• Focus on your heart center, located to the right of your heart in the middle of your chest.

• Tap your heart area with your fingertips as fast, slow, hard, soft, long, or as little as you like.

• The more you use this technique, the more effective it becomes in reducing high levels of stress, in the moment.

Reflect

• When using this practice in moments of calm, it isn't very impactful.

• In moments of suffering, it serves as an anchor of attention linking the mind and body in the here and now.

(2.) SELF-COMPASSION

Learn

Self-compassion is an emergent and ever-changing intra-active process. The way people make sense of the environment, sensory input, internal/external stimuli, etc....determines how they might administer self-compassion. For example, when a thermostat registers the temperature, the next step is dependent on that data. Likewise, in self-compassion, mindful awareness is how one registers their internal temperature and self-kindness is the infinite ways one might respond to themselves with warmth and tenderness.

Embodied action is the stuff people do with their bodies that reflects thought, intention, and planning. The stuff people do with their bodies is proof that they perceive, and also a way of grounding thinking in the present moment. This is especially relevant to teens struggling with chronic and/or terminal illness. When turning inward, truly recognizing needs, desires, views, and beliefs about the world emerges. Resulting action tends to yield powerful outcomes because it is based on grounded cognition, clear perception, and involves embodiment. By embodying action oriented toward the self, with attuned tenderness toward alleviating suffering, everything changes. It is developmentally atypical for teens to explore this existential and metaphysical concept, however, severe illness is an imprisonment of suffering that changes a person's outlook on life.

Help your teen see that self-compassion is the ultimate marriage, or unification with the self, that heals and prepares the soul for life after death. When teens practice self-compassion, they begin cultivating oneness by recognizing themselves and tending to embodied suffering. For healthy teens, initiating self-compassion practice is a lifelong practice that unfolds with development and experience. For teens who are ill, this process is accelerated and may result in rapid change when embraced.

Practice

Discuss these ideas with your teen:

- Embodiment is how our soul, mental, emotional experiences are carried in our bodies. Embodiment can refer to the metaphoric "container" that holds us in the present moment.
- The human mind is always making sense of the environment, and literally changes with new experiences and as new information becomes available.
- We bring meaning to interactions between us and our environment, where the environment can be defined as:
  - The atmosphere and climate.
  - Other people and animals.
  - The internal environment, that is the Self.

- When attention, intention, affect, and insight are all focused inward on an engaged interaction with self (self-empathy) with the purpose of tending to suffering (self-compassion), the ultimate witness and experience of Self can emerge.
- The experience of Self is different from that of self, as it involves unification with the Divine aspects of the Soul.

Reflect

- Help your teen connect their struggle with suffering at such a high degree with mortality and the ultimate connection with Self, the part that is everlasting, interconneted, and fully supported.

- Practicing self-compassion when suffering from terminal illness and facing end of life at a young age may promote enlightenment, and therefore some guidance from an experienced practitioner in self-compassion is recommended.

③ ENDURANCE

Learn

Suffering with chronic and terminal illness is an endurance activity. It begs your teen to power on when there is no gas left. It demands energy after sapping all the reserves. And just when it seems like there is nothing left to give to illness, teens find it somewhere. The following inventory is a self-reflective practice aimed at identifying and cultivating endurance in the face of prolonged and intense suffering.

Practice

Invite your teen to complete the worksheet that follows when encountering various events. An event can include any or all of the following:

- A medical procedure

- An outing

- A visit with a friend or family member

- A trip

- Going to school or an after-school activity

- Entertainment

Encourage your teen to rate their energy level at the beginning and end of each activity.

Reflect

- This self-reflective inventory helps sick teens in cultivating mindful awareness about their energy level.

- Being able to modulate energy is one way of conserving it when low or compromised by illness.

- Mindful awareness is the first step to self-compassion and channeling energy toward healing and integration.

- Another step is in applying self-kindness, which for sick teens may involve setting boundaries, and not attending events that will drain their energy excessively.

- This practice is helpful in initiating increased endurance, however, it will likely become automatic for your teen soon after introduction.

* WORKSHEET *
ENDURANCE LOG

Date	Event	Energy level at beginning	Energy level at the end of the event	Net gain or loss

4. END-OF-LIFE BUCKET LIST

Learn

The Make-A-Wish® Foundation honors the end of life wishes of sick kids and makes them happen every 37 minutes of every day because they believe a "wish experience is a game changer."[4]

Practice

- Prioritize making the wishes and bucket list items of sick teens become a reality.

- Other than medical limitations and procedures, place the wishes of sick teens over other experiences and obligations.

- Ask your sick teen what they want to experience. Invite them to share their wishes.

Reflect

- Are any wishes possible?

- If any wishes were granted, were they game-changing? If so, how?

- Is it indulgent or necessary to grant the wishes of sick teens? If so, how?

---

4   http://wish.org/about-us

(5.) WORKING WITH PAIN

Learn

Much of suffering lies in the second arrow (previously discussed in Chapter 3). The Buddha described the effects of being hit by an arrow begin with the physical and psychological pain of the injury but don't stop there. The effects deepen with the judgments and beliefs that accompany the suffering. The following practice is guidance for you to help your teen turn toward the pain, with the purpose of becoming mindful of the second arrow so action can be taken to eliminate it.

Practice

Use the following script:

- Take a deep breath into your belly.

- Feel it enter your nose, and inflate your chest.

- When you exhale, intentionally send suffering outward through your mouth.

- After three breaths like this, shift your attention and tune directly into the pain and suffering.

- Focus on the site of physical suffering and/or emotional suffering.

- I invite you to truly register the thoughts, feelings, sensations, and beliefs that surface as you tune directly and deeply into this moment of suffering.

- Notice and speak whatever comes to mind, and I will record it. [Write down everything your teen says. Do not say anything, just receive the associations, memories, and observations they report.]

- When you are ready, and feel you have felt the full effects of your suffering and the second arrows that come with it, take three more deep cleansing belly breaths.

- With each exhale through your mouth, release your suffering as much as possible.

- When you are ready, return to the room.

Reflect

- This is a very draining exercise and is not recommended on days when medical procedures are taking place.

- If and when your teen is ready, explore the second arrows they reported that you recorded for them.

- Explore any faulty thinking and logical fallacies that may be a second arrow.

(7.) SELF-COMPASSIONATE DYING

Learn

For some people, being confronted with death reveals lessons, truths, and a certain level of clarity that empowers all who touch the dying. This is true regardless of age, yet doesn't happen for everyone. It is a choice to approach each moment with open eyes or avoidance. The degree to which dying teens open directly to death can influence the ease with which they transition to the next realm.

Practice

- Straining and resisting death is a second arrow.

- As a person melts into the end of life, accepting the terminus of the body, calm acceptance and loving allowance can arise.

- Inspire your teen with stories of other people transitioning peacefully to the next realm, not because they want to and choose to, but because they accept this life as it is.

- Death is scary when we don't know what to expect. Help your teen imagine death and beyond in a way that is comforting to them.

Reflect

- The self-compassion in this practice resides in mindfully accepting and turning toward dying and end of life, rather than resisting it.

- Imagining and opening to death is a profound act of self-kindness that embodies love and courage at the same time.

- This practice contributes to the unification of dying teens with the Self, in preparation for the end of life.

- Approaching the end of life with mindful awareness, self-kindness, and embracing common humanity encapsulates wholesome and self-compassionate dying.

8. DEATH: THE GREATEST TEACHER OF LIFE

Learn

The joy of death is a very real possibility for those who surrender to it as a teacher of how to live. The Mahabharata's Yudhistara said, "The most wondrous thing in the world is that all around us people can be dying and we don't believe it can happen to us." Coming into contact with death directly points to how to cultivate an appreciation for the wondrous miracle that is life. It isn't easy and doesn't come directly, however, you can influence your teen in this direction by demonstrating how life and death go together as ends of one spectrum. We each live along a spectrum of time, space, and experience. By facing death directly, people open to the deepest life lessons. Death opens us to the preciousness and precariousness of life. When appreciating the fullness of life with complete mindfulness, experiences ease, anger has no place, and vitality comes to the fore. This is the gift teacher death offers in the package of radical aliveness. According to Ram Dass, how we spend each moment is a rehearsal for death. This wisdom shows us how the approach of death can be a teacher to open fully to living.

Practice

• Opening to the end of life enables terminally ill teens to access the freedom of living in the moment fully and completely.

• When faced with nearing death, this truth becomes clearer and every moment of life can be lived fully or resisted with fear. Making this choice coincides with accepting death as the greatest teacher ever.

Reflect

• What has the end of life been teaching your teen?

• Does your teen find any comfort in seeing death as a teacher?

(9.) WHY ARE YOU HERE?

Learn

Eastern wisdom traditions proclaim that the soul chooses its purpose and mission before being born. For this practice, invite your teen to self-reflect about why they are here. They may already know what their purpose is, and it may reflect in their values, a mission, or an objective they hold. For others, it may be a stretch to figure this out, and that's okay. Surrendering to not knowing is an honorable end-of-life lesson.

Practice

Invite teens to reflect upon their life's mission.

- What is your life's purpose?

- What values do you hold that you'd like to impart to the world?

- Is there some change you would like to effect somewhere or somehow? (Near or far; in your family, community, country, or the world?)

- Do you see any reason for your suffering?

- When people find meaning in their suffering, challenges, trials, and tribulations, it tends to change the quality of the suffering. Has that happened for you? If so, how? If not, can you see yourself finding meaning in your suffering?

Reflect

- While most teens aren't suffering with illness and contemplating the end of their lives, there are others who have done so before your teen. Explore the role models like Ryan White, for example, who changed the way we treat people with AIDS by living the end of his life with purpose.

- Are there any other teen role models for living the end of life with purpose you can find to help your teen find the common humanity element of self-compassion?

Conclusion

Taking time to cultivate self-compassion is dependent on one's commitment to themselves. It is my sincere hope that through learning how to light the spark of self-compassion in your teen, that you also become invested in fanning the fire in yourself. Cultivating self-compassion and compassion in families, classrooms, and clinics has the power to change the world, by creating stronger, wiser, more caring and capable people. When adult caregivers prioritize self-compassion for the teens in their lives, it is a step forward in mitigating Educational Trauma, and its effects. Self-compassion practices also harness self-healing modalities and properties, making it essential to living a healthy life.

References

For your convenience, you may download a PDF version of the worksheets in this book from our dedicated website: go.pesi.com/Gray

Altucher, J., & Altucher, C. A. (2014). *The power of no: Because one little word can bring health, abundance, and happiness.* CA: Hay House.

Anda, R. F., & Filetti, V. J. (1997). Adverse Childhood Experiences (ACE) Study: Leading Determinants of Health. *Center for Disease Control.* doi:10.1037/e604202012-012.

Ayres, A. J. (2005). *Sensory integration and the child: Understanding hidden sensory challenges* (25th Anniversary ed.). Los Angeles,, CA: Western Psychological Services.

Bibeau, M., Dionne, F., & Leblanc, J. (2015). Can compassion meditation contribute to the development of psychotherapists' empathy? A review. *Mindfulness, 7*(1), 255–263. doi:10.1007/s12671-015-0439-y.

Blesser, B. (2007). The seductive (yet destructive) appeal of loud music. *EContact! 9.4 Perte Auditive Et Sujets Connexes/Hearing (Loss) and Related Issues.* Retrieved December 24, 2015, from http://www.blesser.net/downloads/eContact%20Loud%20Music.pdf

Brach, T. (2012). *True refuge: Finding peace and freedom in your own awakened heart.* New York, NY: Bantam Books.

Brown, B. (2012). *Daring greatly: How the courage to be vulnerable transforms the way we live, love, parent, and lead.* New York, NY: Gotham Books.

Centers for Disease Control and Prevention. (2014, November 12). LGBT Youth. Retrieved March 31, 2016, from http://www.cdc.gov/lgbthealth/youth.htm

Csikszentmihalyi, M. (1990). *Flow: The psychology of optimal experience.* New York, NY: Harper & Row.

Dąbrowski, K. (1964). *Positive disintegration.* Boston, MA: Little, Brown.

Delaney, T., & Hamrick, M. C. (2014). *Building social skills for autism, sensory processing disorders and learning disabilities: Over 105 strategies, activities and sensory tools for children and adolescents.* Eau Claire, WI: PESI Publishing and Media.

Diamond, L. M. (2008). *Sexual fluidity: Understanding women's love and desire.* Cambridge, MA: Harvard University Press.

Dunn, E. W., Aknin, L. B., & Norton, M. I. (2008). Spending money on others promotes happiness. *Science, 319*(5870), 1687–1688. doi:10.1126/science.1150952

Dweck, C. S. (2006). *Mindset: The new psychology of success.* New York, NY: Random House.

Eich, J. (2015). *Dialectical behavior therapy skills training with adolescents: A practical workbook for therapists, teens & parents.* Eau Claire, WI: PESI Publishing and Media.

Fraser, J. M. (2015). *Teaching bullies: Zero tolerance on the court or in the classroom.* Charleston, SC: Motion Press.

Gardner, H. (1993). *Multiple intelligences: The theory in practice.* New York, NY: Basic Books.

Garland, T. (2014). *Self-regulation interventions and strategies: Keeping the body, mind and emotions on task in children with autism, ADHD or sensory disorders.* Eau Claire, WI: PESI Publishing and Media.

Germer, C. K. (2009). *The mindful path to self-compassion: Freeing yourself from destructive thoughts and emotions.* New York, NY: Guilford Press.

Gilbert, P. (2009). *The compassionate mind: A new approach to life's challenges.* Oakland, CA: New Harbinger Press.

Goldstein, E. (2012). *The now effect: How this moment can change the rest of your life.* New York, NY: Atria Books.

Goldstein, L. S. (1997). *Teaching with love: A feminist approach to early childhood education.* New York: Peter Lang Pub.

Goleman, D. (1996). *Emotional intelligence.* New York, NY: Bantam Books.

Goleman, D. (2006). *Social intelligence: The new science of human relationships.* New York, NY: Bantam Books.

Goleman, D., & Ekman, P. (2007, June 12). Three kinds of empathy. Retrieved December 31, 2015, from http://www.danielgoleman.info/three-kinds-of-empathy-cognitive-emotional-compassionate/

Goulston, M. (2010). *Just listen: Discover the secret to getting through to absolutely anyone.* New York, NY: American Management Association.

Gray, P. (2013). *Free to learn: Why unleashing the instinct to play will make our children happier, more self-reliant, and better students for life.* New York, NY: Basic Books.

Greenland, S. K. (2010). *The mindful child: How to help your kid manage stress and become happier, kinder, and more compassionate.* New York, NY: Free Press.

Halifax, J. (2012). A heuristic model of enactive compassion. *Current Opinion in Supportive and Palliative Care, 6*(2), 228–235. doi:10.1097/spc.0b013e3283530fbe

Halifax, J. (2013). G.R.A.C.E. for nurses: Cultivating compassion in nurse/patient interactions. *JNEP Journal of Nursing Education and Practice, 4*(1), 121–128. doi:10.5430/jnep.v4n1p121

Hillman, C., Pontifex, M., Raine, L., Castelli, D., Hall, E., & Kramer, A. (2009). The effect of acute treadmill walking on cognitive control and academic achievement in preadolescent children. *Neuroscience, 159*(3), 1044–1054. doi:10.1016/j.neuroscience.2009.01.057

Hölzel, B. K., Carmody, J., Vangel, M., Congleton, C., Yerramsetti, S. M., Gard, T., & Lazar, S. W. (2011). Mindfulness practice leads to increases in regional brain gray matter density. *Psychiatry Research: Neuroimaging, 191*(1), 36–43. doi:10.1016/j.pscychresns.2010.08.006

Horwitz, K. (2008). *White chalk crime: The real reason schools fail.* Charleston, SC: BookSurge.

Iacoboni, M. (2009). *Mirroring people: The science of empathy and how we connect with others.* New York, NY: Picador.

Kaufman, J. C., & Beghetto, R. A. (2009). Beyond big and little: The four c model of creativity. *Review of General Psychology, 13*(1), 1–12. doi:10.1037/a0013688.

Kaufman, S. B. (2013). *Ungifted: Intelligence redefined.* New York, NY: Basic Books.

Krieger, T., Altenstein, D., Baettig, I., Doerig, N., & Holtforth, M. G. (2013). Self-compassion in depression: Associations with depressive symptoms, rumination, and avoidance in depressed outpatients. *Behavior Therapy, 44*(3), 501–513. doi:10.1016/j.beth.2013.04.004

Levine, S. (1982). *Who dies? An investigation of conscious living and conscious dying.* Garden City, NY: Anchor Press/Doubleday.

Lichtman, G. (2014). *EdJourney: A roadmap to the future of education.* San Francisco, CA: Jossey-Bass.

Mahler, M. S., Pine, F., & Bergman, A. (1975). *The psychological birth of the human infant: Symbiosis and individuation.* New York, NY: Basic Books.

McCraty, R., Atkinson, M., Tomasino, D., & Bradley, R. T. (2009). The coherent heart: Heart-brain interactions, psycho-physiological coherence, and the emergence of system-wide order. Integral Review, 5, 10–115.

McCraty, R., & Zayas, M. A. (2014). Cardiac coherence, self-regulation, autonomic stability, and psychosocial well-being. *Frontiers in Psychology Front. Psychol., 5.* doi:10.3389/fpsyg.2014.01090

McGonigal, K. (2013, June). How to make stress your friend. Retrieved March 7, 2016, from http://www.ted.com/talks/kelly_mcgonigal_how_to_make_stress_your_friend?language=en.

McGonigal, K. (2015). *The upside of stress: Why stress is good for you, and how to get good at it.* New York, NY: Avery, a member of Penguin Random House.

Michaelson, J. (2014, June 17). How the LGBT Experience Will Transform the Practice of Mindfulness. Retrieved May 28, 2016, from http://www.huffingtonpost.com/jay-michaelson/how-the-lgbt-experience-w_b_5499928.html

Mock, J. (2014). *Redefining realness: My path to womanhood, identity, love & so much more.* New York, NY: Atria Books.

Neff, K. (2011). *Self-compassion: Stop beating yourself up and leave insecurity behind.* New York, NY: William Morrow.

Oaklander, M. (2016, March 16). The science of crying. Retrieved March 27, 2016, from http://time.com/4254089/science-crying/?xid=newsletter-brief.

Orloff, J. (1996). *Second sight.* New York, NY: Warner Books.

Reck, J. (2009). Homeless gay and transgender youth of color in San Francisco: "No one likes street kids"—Even in the Castro. *Journal of LGBT Youth, 6*(2-3), 223–242. doi:10.1080/19361650903013519

Reznick, C. (2009). *The power of your child's imagination: How to transform stress and anxiety into joy and success.* New York, NY: Penguin Group.

Rifkin, J. (2009). *The empathic civilization: The race to global consciousness in a world in crisis.* New York, NY: J.P. Tarcher/Penguin.

Rinpoche, T., & Swanson, E. (2012). *Open heart, open mind: Awaking the power of essence love.* New York, NY: Harmony Books.

Robinson, K., & Aronica, L. (2015). *Creative schools: The grassroots revolution that's transforming education.* New York, NY: Viking.

Rogers, C. R. (1967). *On becoming a person: A therapist's view of psychotherapy.* London, UK: Constable.

Rogers, C. R., & Farson, R. E. (1957). *Active listening.* Chicago, IL: Industrial Relations Center, the University of Chicago.

Saltzman, A. (2014). *A still quiet place: A mindfulness program for teaching children and adolescents to ease stress and difficult emotions.* Oakland, CA: New Harbinger Press.

Salzberg, S. (2002). *Lovingkindness: The revolutionary art of happiness.* Boston, MA: Shambhala.

Schwarz, A. (2013, December 14). The selling of attention deficit disorder. Retrieved March 21, 2016, from http://www.nytimes.com/2013/12/15/health/the-selling-of-attention-deficit-disorder.html?src=me&ref=general&_r=1

Seligman, M. E., Steen, T. A., Park, N., & Peterson, C. (2005). Positive psychology progress: Empirical validation of interventions. *American Psychologist, 60*(5), 410-421. doi:10.1037/0003-066x.60.5.410

Shanker, S. (2013). *Calm, alert, and learning: Classroom strategies for self-regulation.* Don Mills, Ontario: Pearson.

Shapiro, F. (2001). *Eye movement desensitization and reprocessing: Basic principles, protocols, and procedures* (Second ed.). New York, NY: Guilford Press.

Siegel, D. J. (2012). *Pocket guide to interpersonal neurobiology: An integrative handbook of the mind.* New York, NY: W.W. Norton.

Siegel, D. J. (2013). *Brainstorm: The power and purpose of the teenage brain.* New York, NY: Tarcher/Penguin.

Siegel, D. J., & Bryson, T. P. (2011). *The whole-brain child: 12 revolutionary strategies to nurture your child's developing mind.* New York, NY: Delacorte Press.

Simons, D. J., & Chabris, C. F. (1999). Gorillas in our midst: Sustained inattentional blindness for dynamic events. *Perception, 28*(9), 1059–1074. doi:10.1068/p2952

Thomas, P. L., Carr, P. R., Gorlewski, J. A., & Porfilio, B. J. (2015). *Pedagogies of kindness and respect: On the lives and education of children.* New York, NY: Peter Lang USA.

Troly-Curtin, M. (1912). *Phrynette married.* Toronto: Macmillan of Canada. United Nations High Commission on Human Rights. (1989). *Fact sheet, the rights of the child* (Rep. No. 10). doi:http://www.ohchr.org/Documents/Publications/FactSheet10rev.1en.pdf

Vingerhoets, A. J. (2013). *Why only humans weep: Unravelling the mysteries of tears.* Oxford: Oxford University Press.

Winnicott, D. W. (1964). *The child, the family, and the outside world.* Reading, MA: A Merloyd Lawrence Book Addison Wesley Publishing.

Zylowska, L. (2012). *The mindfulness prescription for adult ADHD: An eight-step program for strengthening attention, managing emotions, and achieving your goals.* Boston, MA: Trumpeter.